Praise for:
The Warzone PTSD Survivors Guide

Harvey Diamond
#1 Best Selling Author of the fastest selling
Health Book of all time:
"Fit For Life".

As a 45 year Physical Hygiene researcher
I have helped people from all over the world to
achieve optimal health. For 20 of those years I
did not know that I had a deadly time bomb
percolating in my own body.

As a Vietnam Veteran I had been doused
with Agent Orange without knowing it. After
its 20 year incubation period I received the
horrible news that I had Agent Orange induced
Peripheral Neuropathy. This was 20 years after I
returned home from war. I have spent many
years researching the physical & mental issues
that poor health can cause. In my case a
warzone brought me into deadly contact with
Agent Orange which I can't do anything to
erase. What I could do was outlive the death

sentence I was told to expect. I was told that within five years I would be in a wheelchair and more than likely dead. I was told that I would have horrible pain until the end.

That was 25 years ago. Here I am living pain free never having taken a drug. On top of that I do not live in a wheelchair. This was due to my living a super healthy lifestyle that I had begun 20 years before I knew anything about the Agent Orange time bomb.

Many other veterans I have come into contact with were also poisoned. In many this poison also percolated for years without them knowing that they had such a dangerous problem. For many years the poison had no name. It is now called Post Traumatic Stress Disorder. This is another insidious poison. It is a poison of the mind.

What I really appreciate about Don Parent's **Warzone PTSD Survivors Guide** is that it not only addresses PTSD in an easy to understand way, he also gives specific steps on how to live a healthy life with it.

The part that is exciting to me is his understanding of the physical ramifications of PTSD. Substance Abuse & PTSD are often co-occurring which is physically debilitating.

Don has a clear understanding of Physical Hygiene, which he now practices as the next stage in his recovery. You can't heal the mind without also healing the body. In Don's words, "You can't transport a healthy brain around in a wheelbarrow full of horse manure."

You will find his chapter "Physical Hygiene- Body, Heal Thyself," invaluable to your total recovery.

Harvey Diamond
Author of:
- Fit For Life
- Fit For Life – A New Beginning
- Living Health
- Eat For Life
- Living Without Pain
- Fit For Life – Not Fat For Life
- And several others.......

Don's Guide puts PTSD into a perspective that only a Veteran of War could write.

By combining Mental & Physical Healing he gives you important tools for the rest of your life.

Col. (Ret) Dr Ronald Sparks

"As a Vietnam Veteran (who has dealt with his own issues of Post-Traumatic Stress over the years) and as an Army Chaplain (who has provided counseling and care to returning combat arena veterans and continues to do so in a retirement status), I have found Don Parent's Book ("Warzone PTSD Survivors Guide") an insightful, inspirational and indispensable resource. "The Warzone PTSD Survivors Guide" brings a practical and personal perspective on a long overlooked and rarely discussed foundation of the negative effects of war on those who have served in combat arenas as well as the societal fragmentation resulting from those experiences. Anyone reading this book will expose themselves to a life-changing philosophy which, if put into practice, can result in health, hope and healing."

The Rev. Dr. Ronald A. Sparks,
Minister,
United Church of Christ/Chaplain
United States Army Reserve (Ret).

Dedication

This book is dedicated to my wife of 45 years Ginger who has had to deal with PTSD by contact. She has been my best friend through all the ups and downs. We were married on my R&R and I can't believe she stuck with me through what PTSD & War threw at us.

This is fun. I get to do a shout out to our daughters Leah & Kari and their awesome husbands Giovanni Buccarelli & Joe Hassey.

I also get to send my love to my granddaughters Hailey Parent-Buccarelli and Hensley Hassey.

Thanks go to my mom Marilyn Parent, my sister Marcia Helton and her husband Thor Helton for their support and positive input.

I will never forget my good friend Sgt. Lonnie Lebambarb who died next to me during my last day of fighting - Tet Offensive 1968.

I must mention the great support of my Pastor Colonel (Ret.) Dr. Ron Sparks. His work with veterans and everyone he helps through sickness and hard times is amazing.

I also want to thank Jerry and Michelle Dorris of www. AuthorSupport.Com for their cover art and my Editor Mike Valentino: www.editor-ghostwriter.com

To all the men and women Veterans of all services and all wars!

The

Warzone

PTSD Survivors

Guide

Vets Helping Vets

Donald G. Parent Jr

Disabled Vet and PTSD Survivor!

This Guide is backed by our Website:

Medical Disclaimer
Copyright
Page

The information in this guide is the result of years of research and living with Post Traumatic Stress Disorder by the author. The information in this book, by necessity, is of a general nature and not a substitute for an evaluation or treatment by a competent medical specialist. If you believe that you are in need of medical interventions please see a medical practitioner as soon as possible.

For Emergencies

Also to learn more:
WWW.PTSDHotline.Com

Library of Congress Cataloging-in-
Publication Data is available upon request.
Printed in the United States

Cover Design by
Jerry Dorris
www.authorsupport.com

Editing by
Mike Valentino
editor-ghostwriter.com

Formatting by:
Thomas Harwick
thomasharwick.com

Intel Hell

We were ordered to move in the middle of the
night,
The enemy was there if our Intel was right,
Our Orders read;
"Take out the bunkers, destroy hiding places."
They said;
"Toss your grenades. Use all your might!"
"Our Intel is good. It is time for a fight!"

The smoke finally cleared,
Everything became quiet,
Was that crying we heard?
We were disturbed by it,

Our enemy crawled out of tiny little spaces,
Only mothers and children with blood on their
faces!

By:
Don Parent
True event that happened to his unit!

Most causes of PTSD are traumatic events
perpetrated upon someone. It could be rape,

child molestation, spousal abuse or a number of other things.

In the case of Warzone PTSD it can very likely be caused by what we are forced to do to others. In many cases the orders we were asked to carry out did cause powerful traumas all their own.

Warzone PTSD Survivors Guide
Table of Contents

Part 1

Chapter 1: Living with Warzone Post Traumatic Stress Disorder
- What is Warzone PTSD?
- Are you alone?
- How did I get Warzone PTSD?
- What is a Normal Life?

Chapter 2: Symptoms & Reactions:
- Common Symptoms
- Ethics Type Questions
- Other Causes of PTSD
- PTSD Squared
- Types of Therapy

Chapter 3: What's the Next Step? Do Something! Do Not Hide!!!
- What's Next?
- Self-Evaluation. Do I have PTSD?
- More PTSD Symptoms & Therapies
- Do not hide!!!

- Red Flags

Chapter 4: My Personal Recovery
- How did I become a Warzone PTSD Survivor?
- Learning to work with the VA

Chapter 5: VA Benefits
- Falling through the cracks!
- VA Benefits & PTSD
- Important Steps to take for VA Benefits
- Sharing Information
- DD-214 and other paperwork
- Travel Pay, VIC ID Card & more

Part 2
Chapter 6: The Mental Muscle: Self-Hypnosis, Meditation, & More
- Life in the fast lane
- Having a calm mind
- Using Self-Hypnosis
- The Subconscious
- PTSD & Transcendental Meditation

Chapter 7: Physical Health: Body Heal, Thyself!

- Treating the whole person
- Integrative Medicine
- Positive Steps
- Positive Thinking
- Mood Boosting Super Foods

Chapter 8: The Wrap-Up

- Smoothing out your road
- Staying consistent
- Your Default Day
- Final Steps and Check List

Part 1

Chapter 1

Living With
Warzone Post Traumatic Stress Disorder

Let me start this Guide with a little disclaimer-

My name is Don Parent. I am not a professional writer nor do I have any training in psychiatry. I am a disabled Vietnam Veteran living with PTSD. If any of this Guide seems disjointed or repetitive just chalk it up to my having PTSD! Throw in a little ADD and here I am!

I have used two acronyms already and we are only in the first paragraphs. I will try to stay away from using too many of them but it may be hard to do with this subject matter.

TBI's & Other Problems

There are many other issues such as Traumatic Brain Injuries that cause our returning vets serious problems. Soldiers with TBI's have some symptoms in common with PTSD due to the fact that they easily can be co-occurring. What caused the TBI can be traumatic in many ways. The TBI is physical where PTSD is caused by severe mental stress.

In this Guide we will be dealing with PTSD. There is a ton of information about TBI's available to you on the Internet.

See our TBI's Message Board at:
http://www.ptsdhotline.com/forum/forum.php

Living a PTSD kind of life

Have I made mistakes in my life? Of course I have. Everyone does. I don't blame all my screw-ups or struggles on PTSD. Just some of them! War and PTSD did cause a huge re-routing of the life I had hoped to live. I am sure I would have made many mistakes without PTSD; however my war experiences and the PTSD that resulted sidetracked my life into a runaway train ride fueled by adrenaline, confusion, anger, and mistrust for all authority.

PTSD was and still is my rebellion against society

I should say a rebellion against a government that played fast and loose with the hundreds of thousands of young expendables they sent off to war. Our government is supposed to reflect society and its needs but more often than not it doesn't end up working out that way.

It took me decades to come to terms with all of this and to understand that thousands of other veterans who had come before me shared my struggles.

This Guide is not a 1000 page tome that only a Ph.D. would understand. It is condensed down into something that veterans of all wars will relate to. The steps involved in this PTSD Survivors Guide are simple. If you truly wish to live a life not ruled by PTSD, then keep reading.

Everything in this book comes from my struggles over the past 45 years living with PTSD, substance abuse, anger and all the problems a War Zone will cause a young mind.

Becoming a PTSD Survivor is not a Race

In this Guide we will cover a number of topics that will help you live a better life. It is important to understand that this is not a race. Becoming a Warzone PTSD survivor is a progression. There are several main ingredients that PTSD survivors have that veterans losing the struggle do not.

One is an ingredient that I had first heard about from Dr. Wayne Dyer a number of years ago. It is called:

The Power of Intention

Now I am not writing this guide to promote Dr. Wayne Dyer or any of the other well-known doctors or psychiatrists who I mention in these pages. However, I have gleaned great ideas from many of them. I had to dig around for many years to snag bits and pieces that I was able to puzzle together much later.

Intention stuck in my mind but I didn't put it into use with regard to PTSD until much later. I was still living with the PTSD roller coaster ride but the thrills no longer held any fun or excitement for me. In fact, I was getting extremely tired of the highs and lows that this type of life was causing me. I needed to have a carpenter's level surgically attached to the top of my teeter-tottering head.

I finally realized that I had been flip-flopping around for years. I now understand that I had this thing called PTSD - Post Traumatic Stress Disorder. Talk about a fish out of water feeling!

I wasn't stupid and I did have a lot of info swimming around in my mind. I began to reel the important thoughts in instead of just plain rolling around the deck and bouncing off the bulkheads.

I started thinking of how I could use intention to survive. I began playing with the word "Intention" and trying to use it to work on what was happening to me. I knew I had to put some specific steps together to finally get over the war. An extremely powerful word popped out at me. Once I really thought about this word I realized it would be the key to changing me from a causality of war to becoming a Warzone PTSD survivor. The word was Proactive. You will see it in this Guide many times.

It is an action word that will easily change you from a lost soul into a War Zone PTSD survivor. This guide will give you specific tools and steps to use once you decide to get your life back on track. Until you become proactive in your recovery you will just be another fish out of water.

When it comes to PTSD, becoming Proactive is the Power of Intention on steroids! You need to say, "Enough is

Enough." It is time to do something productive. You need to say, "I intend to get out of this cave that PTSD has put me in. No more hiding!" Hopefully the act of cracking the cover of this Guide is that all-important first step for you! Having a Guide like this will help you. There was nothing like it when the Vietnam Vets came home. Believe me if I could become a Warzone PTSD survivor without this Guide I know without a doubt that you can with it. The difference is that my recovery took over 40 years. If you follow the specific steps in this guide you can change years to months.

The reason I mention Specific Tools & Steps is that one of the problems many face related to PTSD is a sporadic lifestyle. Sufferers live in a confusion of highs and lows that can seem like bipolar problems. That is why things like grounding techniques are such an important tool.

By giving you specific tools and steps in a reasonable progression I hope to take much of the guess work out of it for you.

Are there other ways to deal with PTSD? Maybe! However this progression has worked extremely well for me and I see it working for all the other veterans that I am in contact with. By following the steps outlined in this guide I also received 100% service connected benefits. I cannot guarantee this for you. Not everyone gets monetary benefits, however your chances are improved immensely. I back this up with steps to take if you are denied.

The Veterans Administration: Let's step back into my past:

A number of years after my return from Vietnam I began going to the Veterans Administration to seek help. I knew things were different with me. I just didn't know what those changes meant. I no longer wanted to go to college for engineering as I had before Vietnam. I didn't know what I wanted to do but it wasn't sitting at a desk or drawing board. Sitting still was something I could no longer seem to do.

In the early days going to the VA was an interesting experience. Not good interesting! It was not the VA of today. The VA was much more confusing than it is today. It still can be confusing. The people at the VA were as confused as the Vets were. They didn't know what to do with the Vietnam Vets coming in acting goofy and smelling like refer madness. We were like hippies on steroids. It was the 1960s after all, but all the marijuana in the world wouldn't calm down our angst and anger.

The VA System was a huge learning curve not only for me but for the VA as well. PTSD was not even an acronym back in those days. If you talk to most VA doctors today they will agree that what they know about PTSD they learned from the Vietnam Veterans. There sure were plenty of us to study and practice on.

It was easy to run away from the VA back then. If it hadn't been for the other Vets that I met at the VA hospitals I wouldn't have kept coming back myself. Talking with vets from all wars over the years gave me answers that I couldn't find anyplace else. There were no books or guides like this one. The term PTSD was still years away. Statements like "Just Suck it Up and Move On" were bandied about by the military establishment. Talk about incredibly bad advice!

I couldn't have become a PTSD survivor without the help of the thousands of vets that I talked to over the years. They were also struggling with their own demons. We struggled and learned together as did the doctors, psychiatrists and psychologists who wanted to help us. They did want to help us, they just didn't know enough back then to do that. It was an important two way street for all of us.

Learning the VA System and coming to terms with my problems took years. I believe that my 45 years of learning will cut many years off of your search for answers. Myself and the many vets that came before you have made practically every mistake possible. Learn from us!

Vets Helping Vet

PTSD in General

There are many types of traumas that can cause PTSD. The reason this book is about Warzone PTSD is simple. That is what caused mine. Through the many years of digging into my problems, I did learn about the other types of causes but being the self-absorbed person that I am I needed to write about the type that affected me.

I was not beaten as a child or raped. I did not live through a horrific accident or any of the other things that some of you may have experienced.

There are a number of things in common with all the causes of PTSD and sufferers who were never in a War Zone can glean important insights into their own issues from reading this guide as well.

I highly recommend that the families and friends of PTSD sufferers, from any cause, dig in and read any information that they can find whether in books, the Internet or from family support groups. The veteran close to you needs your support and understanding.

What is a Warzone PTSD Survivor?

A Warzone PTSD Survivor is not a perfect little robotron that walks around like a zombie never doing anything wrong. A Warzone PTSD Survivor is a complex person who has been traumatized in a Warzone and knows that they have ongoing problems that they must continue to deal with! One of the biggest steps toward becoming a PTSD Survivor is realizing that you have it. It is not like a bad cough or runny nose. You don't all of a sudden say, "Wow, I have PTSD! Pass the Kleenex!"

A Warzone PTSD Survivor has learned who they need to talk to, how to ask for the help that they need and won't let their problems destroy their life or the lives of their family and friends. A PTSD Survivor is a person who wants to succeed in the home, workplace and community. They learn grounding techniques that can stop a downward spiral before it picks up steam.

This guide is written with veterans of all wars in mind. Much of what is in this guide can be useful to people still on active duty as well, however, there are some differences to consider for those still on active duty. I will go into that more later in this guide.

What caused my Warzone PTSD?

I will try to explain the question, "How did I get War Zone PTSD?" as briefly as possible. The sooner we can get on to the steps you need to take to become a PTSD Survivor the better.

I will briefly outline my history before, during, and the aftermath of my Vietnam War experience. I should call it the afterbirth as I became a totally changed person.

This guide isn't about me. It is about what people with War Zone PTSD have in common and how to become a Warzone PTSD Survivor yourself. You will be surprised to find just how many things you share with others that also have been traumatized by war. It is important to understand that:

You Are Not Alone!

I personally know many vets that did not find this out until they were in their fifties and even sixties. They hid out thinking that their problems and invasive thoughts were unique unto themselves. It is extremely relieving once you realize that you have brothers and sisters also traveling this sporadic post war journey. Having someone to talk to that is a kindred spirit is like having a giant weight lifted from your chest.

Substance Abuse

PTSD in many cases is co-occurring with substance abuse. Self-medication is extremely common with people suffering from PTSD!

You can always tell a PTSD Survivor by the way they talk. Instead of saying "I had a drinking problem" they will say "I had a self-medicating problem"! You will understand this more through the following chapters.

To become a PTSD Survivor you will need to take a serious look at the self-medication issues as well. Now don't get nervous. There is a big difference between having a drink or smoke once in a while and having an issue with substance abuse. The abuse of anything is not good for anyone.

An important statement that you will want to memorize is seeking safety! What is safe for you? Can you control a couple of beers or will a few beers send you into a downward spiral? There is a great program at a number of VA's around the country that is for PTSD and Substance Abuse combined. I will talk more about this in later chapters.

My Warzone story in brief

You will find a number of things in my story that you will relate to. Skim through it and you will find some parts that resonate with you. This is very brief. As I have said this guide is not about me. It is about all of us vets pulling together to help each other.

I had an average childhood growing up in Chicago and later the San Fernando Valley of California. I was born in 1945 right at the end of WWII. My dad was in the Navy stationed in Florida and as soon as he was released we moved back to his hometown of Chicago.

We then moved to Southern California. I was going into the 3rd grade.

Out of high school I was hired as a design engineer working on hydraulic and pneumatic systems for military contractors such as Bell Helicopter and Hydraulic Research Corp.

At the age of 18 I got in a little trouble for fist fighting and was placed on probation until my 21st birthday. I couldn't join the service or be drafted because of this. I thought that was an interesting "Catch 22". I couldn't go to war to fight because I was in trouble for fighting! ☺

This actually came around to bite me. I couldn't join the military while on probation. Joining would have given me a chance at a decent MOS (Military Occupation Specialties).

A week after my 21st birthday I received my draft notice. It was now too late to join. By the time I got drafted, in 1966, they needed cannon fodder to throw against the so-called Communist threat. They didn't need guys sitting at a drawing board. This really lowered my chances of getting a decent MOS.

I only had three days to report for duty! The draft notice had been stuck in the bill drawer at my parents' home and we didn't find it until I had only three days to say goodbye, quit my job and report to downtown Los Angeles. From there they bused a bunch of scared Valley Boys up to Fort Ord in Northern California. We acted real tough on the bus to hide our shock and fear of what lay in store for us!

Fort Ord, California

I took all the mental tests that the Army could come up with thinking that I had this whooped. I hoped that with my background in hydraulics and pneumatics I would become an engineer with a nice clean, behind the front lines, uniform. The Army said, "Sorry son, you know nothing about engineering! You are in the infantry now!" That was my first clue of what lay ahead.

Being yanked away from my girlfriend Ginger, getting sheered of my long hair and perforated by a million shots was a real trauma all of its own. In the middle of the night you could hear someone in the olive drab barracks cry out, "I want my mommy!" or something along those lines! This may not be food for PTSD but it was a real shocker none the less.

There I was in basic training. We did the entire crawl in the mud, choke on the gas routine. It did kick my butt into shape though!

Tiger Land

Next I was shoved on a plane and ended up at Fort Polk, Louisiana. Tiger Land, USA! This was aptly named as it turned a bunch of pussy cats into fire breathing fanged predators.

An interesting difference between Fort Ord and Fort Polk was the mud. California mud was nice and squishy when you landed on it. It was even warm!

Fort Polk's mud, in November, was another story all together. When you landed on it, it hurt like hell. Once you broke through the top layer of brown jagged ice you were sucked down into freezing primordial ooze. Drill Sergeants crawled out of this ooze fully formed screaming: "There's only one way off of this island, maggots. That's in a pine box!

They should have filmed, "The Lord of the Rings" movies there. They would have found plenty of extras running around. Drill Sergeants would have made perfect "Orcs." Who needs camouflage makeup when you have all of that baby crap colored mud clinging to every part of your body?

Vietnam

The next thing I knew I was landing in Cam Rahn Bay, Vietnam. The second my foot touched the Vietnamese soil an electrical charge shot straight up though my shiny new jungle boots. There is no way to explain this powerful sensation unless you have been to a Warzone. Your whole body crackles with the adrenaline rush of it all!

Vietnam and Southern California were nothing alike. The sights, sounds and smells assaulted my senses in so many ways that I couldn't soak them up fast enough. I found it extremely exciting. The potential danger in every direction added to the cacophony I was experiencing. It was real heady stuff.

Riding on a convoy through downtown Pleiku on my way to my first unit was a jumble of blowing horns, shopkeepers calling out in their native tongue, exotic women in sexy split up the side dresses and bicycles and motor scooters jumping in and out of traffic like a bunch of wild banshees!

I loved every bit of it. Humphrey Bogart move over we are coming through!

The year I spent in Vietnam was a whirlwind of adrenaline rushes, combat assaults, homesickness, fear and all the other emotions' jumbled together into an exotic soup. It had extreme highs and frightening lows sometimes all in the same hour or day.

All Wars

This book is not only about Vietnam. It is about all the wars and conflicts Governments and big business like to throw at us. They didn't have the term PTSD until long after Vietnam. The other wars called it shell shock, combat fatigue and a number of other things. Some misguided individuals, such as General George Patton even tried to call it cowardice.

There was a terrible incident during WWII when General Patton slapped a soldier with PTSD and called him a coward! The General was rightfully reprimanded. He has since been proven wrong time and time again! How you could slap anyone who had just gone through the horrors of the front lines of WWII, and call them a coward is really wrong on so many levels.

My Uncle Bob Bullot was General Patton's adjutant during this time. He is gone now. That is too bad as I would have loved to talk to him about this.

During my year in Vietnam I received several Purple Hearts. I got wounded 5 or 7 times. I lost track of the amount of wounds I sustained during my last 2 days of fighting. It was during the 1968 Tet Offensive and the Vietnamese mud was hitting the fan. Vietnam mud was interesting in the incredible amount of it they had for us to play in. What is with the military and mud? The Vietnamese mud came with fun things like leeches to add to the thrill of it all.

Leeches! Now there is a word that will get a Vietnam Vet to open up and talk! There is nothing like the sight of a Combat Killing Machine loaded down with grenades and bristling with weaponry running tiptoe through the muddy water crying, "Leeches, Leeches!" Yes that was me! Talk about mini aliens! In my mind they were as big as the one in the movies with that extra set of blood sucking lips that shot out of its face full of teeth!

Yep another movie: "Aliens"! It is interesting that I look back on my Vietnam years as a motion picture. Many of you will relate to this. I can't get my mind around the whole scenario as real life.

The Tet Offensive

The Tet Offensive was one hell of a last few days of fighting for me. The one thing I know for sure, as I sit here in a hard chair typing is that most of my wounds were in my butt. Everyone told me to keep my head down. I did! I forgot to have my ass follow my head. The opposite has been true for many years. There are more jokes in there somewhere. I'll leave them to your imagination. I am sensitive about that part of my body. Most vets hate having their backs exposed while in a crowded room. My friends still ask me, "Don, why are you always scooting your ass into the rear corner seat?"

I ended up with two Purple Hearts. I had received the first during one of the many earlier firefights I was involved in during my tour. Yeah, that one was in the butt as well! ☺

The second Purple Heart I received was for my last days of fighting. I was wounded at least four times in that final two day battle. I lost track. You only get one Purple Heart per battle, I guess, no matter how many times you get shot in the butt. It is considered a blanket Purple Heart although I doubt that it will keep you warm at night. I would have been better served receiving bullet proof BVD's if they wanted to give me anything at all.

During this intense Vietnam year I married my girlfriend Ginger in Hawaii on my R&R (Rest & Recuperation Leave). Six days of bliss and then back to the war. We have now been married for over 45 years as of this writing. She is still my best friend. That is really rare for a PTSD Veteran. More on that later.

All this happened in just one deployment (1 Year). How could that much happen in just one year? You can imagine the layers of trauma our veterans now go through due to multiple deployments. No my wedding was not one of the traumas. Having to go back to Vietnam after six days of bliss however was a real bummer.

I could go on and on about all the hell and horror that I went through during my deployment but this book is about becoming a PTSD and Substance Abuse Survivor. Suffice it to say that I did not have to dig deep to find many instances that cause PTSD. I would rather move quickly on to the steps you will need to take to become a survivor as well.

My Trip Home

The Army saved one last little "Oops! Did I do that?" for my journey home from Vietnam. I was air evacuated out from Cam Rahn Bay with enough open wounds to make me look like Swiss cheese. I landed in the Philippines for a one week layover on my way to Tripler Army Hospital in Hawaii.

After a few days in a ward I was able to walk around and I actually felt pretty good. All my wounds were basically flesh wounds with one bigger through and through bullet hole to my hip. No bones were impacted. I could still walk so they gave me a day pass to go see Manila. I was really excited.

I was stepping up onto a bus when I started feeling really woozy. Everything started spinning. I guess I passed out because I woke up back in the hospital ward. It turned out that with many open wounds the Army had accidentally put me in a hepatitis ward. Yes, I had hepatitis. Well at least now I was in the right ward. The doctors were just planning ahead! ☺

Tripler Hospital, Hawaii

I finally did get to Hawaii but I was not allowed out of my hospital bed for a month. No warm beaches, no "Surfin' Safaris", no "Beach Boys" music, no nothin'! My only thrill was being visited by General Westmoreland's wife. At that time General Westmoreland was the Commander of the Armed Forces in Vietnam. She was really nice to the wounded and brought us cookies and a pleasant smile. I would have much rather hit the beach!

The Aftermath

One of the troubling things that I was told, a number of times, as I was leaving the Army was to keep my mouth shut! They said that I would be better off keeping quiet about my Vietnam experiences. Public opinion was really negative toward the war. I was told things like, "Keep your trap shut! Get a job and move on with your life." This was, by far, the worst advice I have ever received in my life. The worst thing a Vet can do is bury all the negative emotions and hide. I will go more into this in later chapters.

It was time to lead a Normal life! Or was it?

Now there is a ridiculous scenario if there ever was one. Take one young man or woman. Teach them how to kill. Load them full of horrible memories. Addict them to adrenaline rushes, tell them to suck it up, go get a job, and lead a normal life. Now sit back and let the fireworks begin!

At least the Vietnam vets had jobs available to come home to. The vets coming home as of this writing (2012) are treated to a far worse economy. This puts much more stress on an already volatile situation.

I took several jobs over the next three years after my release. I also got into self-medicating with drugs and alcohol. I had not used any drugs before Vietnam but had learned to use drugs and alcohol, there. This was to cope with the war and being so far from home. This is unfortunately extremely common. When you don't know if you will be alive the next day health issues are at the bottom of your list. Smoke, drink, and do drugs! What the hell! I only used my toothbrush to clean my rifle. Who needs fresh breath when your M 16 jams up in a fire fight! How many of you dumped the M16 and scrambled for an M14 when all hell broke loose. The M14 never jammed! Plus it was so big and heavy you could use it as a club or battering ram!

During the first few years of my "normal life" I was constantly looking for thrills and the excitement that I received in war but I didn't get from my jobs. I felt as if I had lost the power that I had felt as a combat infantryman. Some vets go into law enforcement or even re-enlist in the military to get that feeling of "power" back.

After several years of trying to hold it together I exploded and went running into the hills. I speak figuratively but looking back it feels like that is exactly what I did.

This escalated over the next 30 years. I couldn't work for companies or take any orders or direction of any kind. I had zero trust and lived an underground lifestyle hiding from taxes and government regulations. I did many under the table things to feed my family. Many not so good!

All this played hell on my marriage and I am still amazed that my wife Ginger stayed with me. Needless to say Ginger had "PTSD by Contact." It is similar to, but much worse than, second hand smoke. Wives or partners become more like caregivers. Many times that doesn't work out well for them.

Many of you reading this and dealing with PTSD will have had numerous spouses or relationships. This is an extremely common by-product of what war causes. There are many instances of both husband and wife being in the military and deployed at the same time. Many of them have had several deployments to deal with. They then try to live a normal life together. I don't know how they do that. It can be done but the issues involved must be approached head on with a commitment to counseling being mandatory. Otherwise the problems will fester and multiply as ours did.

I went to the VA but did not try very hard. I went more to make Ginger think that I was doing something. I did not dig in and start getting serious counseling until I was in my 50's and 60's. By then my PTSD and Substance Abuse was deeply entrenched!

This is happening far too often. Many vets now coming home are learning to hide their emotions. The military tries to talk to soldiers as they are preparing to leave country at the end of their deployment. They are asked questions relating to their state of mind.

The returning soldiers know that if they ask for help at this juncture they will more than likely be held up in their return home. They will be put into counseling. It is common practice to fake it so that they can go home as quickly as possible. This is the start of sweeping their troubles under the carpet.

Another stumbling block that many soldiers have to deal with involves not wanting PTSD in their permanent record.

They fear that it can cause problems for their continued military careers and also for soldiers or vets hoping to go into law enforcement or jobs like firefighters. If this is a concern to you then learn who you should talk to. It is like anything else in life. You shouldn't run up and down the street telling everyone your personal issues. However, do not stick your head in the sand! Get books like this one. Talk with doctors and other veterans you meet at the VA or Vet Centers. Ask questions. Not every vet will have the right answer for you but use your wits to filter the input. You don't need to give everyone your personal ID information to get answers. In other words asking questions does not go on your permanent record.

Ask me: DonP@PTSDHotline.Com.

I have done years of work and research for my own recovery and now I want to help as many others as I can reach. Asking questions on our message boards is a great way to become proactive in your recovery! Message Boards at PTSDHotline.com: http://www.ptsdhotline.com/forum/forum.php

You may get tired of hearing proactive from me but if I say it enough hopefully you will get it implanted subliminally and won't forget it. It is that important.

I can't think of a stronger piece of information to impart here. I did not start to heal until I got heavily involved in my own recovery. The VA and the Vet Centers now have great programs for PTSD, Substance Abuse, Anger Management, family Issues and more. The professional doctors, psychiatrists, psychologists, and clinicians are legally bound to keep your personal information secure. Don't be afraid to talk to them. Tell them your concerns and ask what steps you should take.

Note: We have backed up this guide with a website: WWW.PTSDHotline.Com

Again our website has message boards where you can ask your questions anonymously if you are concerned about your permanent record. The most important thing for you to realize is that you are not alone. What you are dealing with is shared by many thousands of veterans that have come home before you. What you are feeling is not unique.

Vets Helping Vets
Important Keys to start your Recovery:
- Realizing that you are not alone.
- Doing a serious Self-Evaluation. (See Chapter 3) Could you have PTSD?
- Becoming Proactive in your recovery.
- Going to the VA to Ask Questions.
- Talking to other vets. Ask Questions!
- Finding the program that feels right for you.
- Joining support groups.
- Do not hide! (See Chapter 3)
- Never! Never! Never! Give up on your recovery!

Chapter 2

Symptoms & Reactions
Do you have PTSD?

Common symptoms and reactions experienced by returning war veterans include:

- Hyper-alertness (i.e., difficulty relaxing or feeling safe even in an unthreatening environment) and startled reactions.
- Guilt - The Why Me Question. Why did I live and my buddy didn't?
- Anger (e.g., over command decisions, not being adequately trained, not having necessary equipment, acts committed by the enemy).
- Road Rage.
- Insomnia.
- Difficulty concentrating.
- Recurring thoughts and memories of war experiences.
- Grief and sadness over losses.
- Lack of grief and sadness over losses (disconnect) (e.g., over actions and/or inaction, surviving when others died).

- Impatience and low tolerance for frustrations (e.g., civilian rules may seem irrelevant or meaningless).
- Difficulty connecting with and trusting others, especially those without War Zone experience.
- Anxiety about being re-deployed.
- Trust Issues – We learn to trust our brothers in arms completely. This causes many problems because we look for that trust level with people when we come back to the "normal life". It is an "all or nothing" viewpoint. We have to learn levels of trust all over again. People are shocked when they do a minor infraction and we treat them like they could have gotten us killed.

The items above are all normal responses to the very abnormal events and conditions experienced in war, and they usually diminish over time once the veteran becomes proactive in their recovery. Without proactive counseling Post-traumatic Stress Disorder (PTSD) can become a disabling disorder. Often, people with PTSD have persistent frightening thoughts, memories, and dreams of the terrifying event or events and feel emotionally distant. An event resulting in PTSD can involve experiencing death or dismemberment, in some fashion, and a feeling that one was helpless during that event.

If the PTSD is allowed to percolate these problems can begin to spiral out of control:

- Acting or feeling as if the traumatic event were happening again and again. Also called flash backs.
- Recurring and intrusive memories and/or dreams of the event. This is separate from flash backs. It can be similar to snapshot like photos that pop into the mind at unwanted times.
- Intense distress in response to cues resembling some aspect of the event.
- Efforts to avoid thoughts, feelings, or conversations related to the event. A need to hide.
- Feeling detachment or estrangement from others.
- Difficulty falling or staying asleep.
- Irritability or outbursts of anger.
- Difficulty concentrating.
- Depression

PTSD Soup

A Recipe for Disaster...

- 1 Fresh Young person
- 2 Quarts of War
- 8 Cups Adrenaline
- A Truckload of Assorted Drugs and Alcohol – Use liberally as needed
- Sprinkle on a Large Topping of **Trauma** while serving!

Throw all these ingredients into an M-1 field helmet. No extra heat needed! Stir with an entrenching tool and watch them bubble over the top!

This recipe will strip a young person of their joy for life, their sympathy toward others, their ability to feel deep loss, and many of the other feelings that young people should be allowed to take for granted.

The Ethics Questions

The most surprising thing of all, which took me the longest to understand, is that war *will* strip a young person of their knowledge of what is right and wrong. It totally blurs many of the ethics type questions that we all need to live by for a healthy, happy life.

When you are ordered to kill, which you normally would never do, it blurs things. It gets worse when you watch another GI sneak out to a village at night knowing that he is going to rape a woman and yet you say nothing. This continues to wreak havoc on the ethics questions.

The longer you are in a War Zone the more instances of unethical events will continue to occur. You don't have to actually kill or rape to still feel quilt. Hopefully, for your sake, you still feel that guilt after seeing things like this happen. If you no longer care then a much larger crime has been committed against you.

These things above actually happened to me. Those exact things may not have happened to you but I am sure that you can make a long list of many others that still bother you today.

These are the types of things that we shove down and self-medicate to try to avoid thinking about. These are the types of things that fuel the anger and the disconnection that is a part of PTSD.

This PTSD Survivors Guide is primarily about Warzone PTSD!

Healing from PTSD and substance abuse brought me back to good relationships with my family and friends.

When I say healing I do not use the word curing. A person cannot totally exorcise the traumatic memories that caused the condition but by learning to use the proper mental tools a person can regain control over the way they wish to live their lives. Regaining power and control over your life is a wonderful feeling and worth any amount of effort to get there. Yes it does take work in the form of becoming proactive with your recovery. To become proactive you simply have to want to live a better life. The more you want it the easier your recovery will become. You may experience a number of starts and stops with lengthy downward spirals. That will happen. Make the decision to never give up on your recovery. The downward spirals will become shorter and easier to stop.

Other causes of PTSD

This Guide is about War Zone Post Traumatic Stress Disorder (PTSD). Mine was caused by a War Zone; however there are many other events that can cause PTSD such as:

- A bad accident
- Car or Plane Crash
- Rape or Sexual Molestation
- Child Abuse
- Physical and Mental Abuse
- Losing a loved one
- 9/11 and other large traumatic events
- Earthquake, Hurricane, etc.

People who suffer from PTSD have many things in common regardless of what caused their condition.

This Guide will give you a general overview of PTSD. The causes may be different from yours. The levels of the disorder will be different depending on whether it is caused by one event or many as usually happen in a War Zone and many times with child and spousal abuse type situations as well.

Virtually any trauma, defined as an event that is life-threatening or that severely compromises the physical or emotional well-being of an individual or causes intense fear, can cause PTSD.

Here's a few more:
- Receiving a life-threatening medical diagnosis
- Being the victim of kidnapping or torture
- Exposure to a natural disaster
- Terrorist attack
- Being the victim of a mugging, robbery, or assault
- Involvement in civil conflict

The diagnosis of PTSD currently requires that the sufferer has a history of experiencing a traumatic event as defined here. However, people may develop PTSD in reaction to events that may not qualify as traumatic but can be devastating life events like divorce or unemployment.

In the case of PTSD caused by war the situations more than likely will be in layers of trauma (Complex PTSD). A tour/deployment of duty in a War Zone can have any number of PTSD causing events.

PTSD Squared

This topic will be mentioned several times in this Guide because it is important. Someone may go into a Warzone with a preexisting PTSD condition. It could be something similar to one of the above traumas that happened earlier in their life. Add layers of trauma that can happen in a War Zone on top of that earlier event and you now have PTSD squared!

Multiple layers of trauma can cause a problem in diagnosis and treatment of the condition. This is a good place to explain the difference between Simple PTSD and Complex PTSD.

- **Simple PTSD:** This is a situation where a person lives with one horrific event in their life. It is easy to locate what that event is and to treat it with known therapy techniques. Using the term Simple PTSD does not mean that the one event is less traumatic. Only that by being one event it is much easier to locate and diagnose.
- **Complex PTSD:** Prolonged and Repeated Events
(Note: This is my layman's brief example of this condition).
This condition is caused by multiple PTSD events in a person's lifetime. It could be repeated instances of a similar event as in repeated rapes or child beating events. It could be many events as they occur in a War Zone, especially after repeated deployments. The event or events can become confused due to one event earlier in life coupled with multiple events in a War Zone. Treatment then involves

peeling back the many layers of trauma to determine the best way to deal with this complicated situation.

Types of Therapy:
Either of the above scenarios may well involve several types of treatment. Below are examples of a few:

- Exposure Therapy
- Talk Therapy
- Drug Therapy
- Cognitive-behavioral Therapy
- Anger Management
- Marriage Counseling
- Family Counseling

Note: These therapies will be discussed further in Chapter #3 and are available at most VA Hospitals and/or Vet Centers.

The earlier a person can get involved in treatment after a PTSD event will dramatically reduce the life changing problems caused by bad advice such as **"Sucking It Up"** and pretending nothing happened. Doing that caused me intense problems for over 40 years.

Below is an interesting excerpt from an excellent book. It highlights the problems of "Sucking it UP" and pretending everything is OK:

Excerpt from the book "MEDIC!" by Vietnam veteran and medic Ben Sherman.

"Most of the war stories you've heard, especially the really exciting ones, have likely come from the vivid imaginations of rear echelon guys who never saw a firefight, never spent a day in the jungle, never slept in a rice paddy, never had their stomach turn over as they gawked at the open wound of a guy who bummed a smoke the minute before. Those who witness the raw hysterics of war up close tend to remain very quiet about it, forever. They think about it, you can be sure, but the words can't get around the clog in the chest.

There's a code. If you've really been in it, you don't talk about it. Maybe that hasn't always been such a good idea. We don't talk to each other. We don't talk to loved ones. It stays in the bottle, corked tight. As years passed, some have broken the silence. They've written books, both truth and fiction. A few have made movies, both accurate and not. Vietnam literature shelves in libraries and bookstores bulge with rage, righteous indignation, continued political discontent and who-owes-who. Vietnam poetry steams off the page. There's still a bunch of folks out there doing their yelling about a war we lost almost thirty some years ago.

A fellow vet I once worked with had a T-shirt that read: "Southeast Asia Games, 1963-1975, Second Place." His wit replaced the flesh he had left on China Beach for a cause he still couldn't articulate. Poorly stitched scars ran from his belly to his neck, then around his shoulder. Field scars. Deep ugly raised skin ridges that were hard to look at twice.

There had been no time in a field hospital to make them pretty."

Note: Being a medic in Vietnam or any war is an extremely dangerous MOS. Thank

God for them. I can say that from my personal experiences with medics whether it was helping me or saving the lives of my comrades in arms.

As a Conscientious Objector Ben wouldn't kill for his country but he was willing to die for it. His is a remarkable story of courage and ethics.

Thanks Ben and Welcome Home!

Read his Book!

www.shermanauthor.com

Do Not Bottle Up your Feelings!

That does not mean to let them fly all over the place. In the next chapter we will discuss how important it is to take immediate steps toward regaining control over your own life.

Author's Note: This Guide is a brief overview of my War Zone PTSD. Mine was caused by many horrific events that I witnessed but it serves no purpose for me to list them all. I have dealt with them and now have control over the negative thoughts when they pop up. It is more important to supply you with specific steps that you should take to regain control over your life as well.

If you wish to do more serious research there is in-depth information available on the Internet or in many other medical books.

For those of you who wish to research more I have a website to help you get started. It even has a resource I built to help you search out the new up to date PTSD News Articles from hundreds of newspapers and to search their archives as well. This is a valuable resource that actually took me a lot of time to build so I would get a real kick out of it if any of you use it to help in your recovery.

Let me know if it helps get you good info:

On the website I have also listed some excellent source books. I especially like the "For Dummies" Guide books. They are simple and fun to read. I have used many of them with great results.

Unless you want to become a doctor and do deep research these books are perfect.

DonP@PTSDHotline.Com

WWW.PTSDHotline.Com

Vets Helping Vets

Chapter 3

What's the Next Step?

You or someone close to you must have PTSD or you probably wouldn't be reading this Warzone PTSD Survivors Guide.

What should be done next? The key is to:
Do Something!
Do Not Hide!

Don't hide from the VA! I did and it added 40 extra years to my recovery! This cannot be said enough.

Many of you vets that don't like the VA probably have run into someone or something there that has made you mad. I hear this all the time. It is really easy for vets with PTSD to get upset. When you let it become a barrier to your future you are not teaching the VA a lesson, you are shafting yourself.

Do not let other people's barriers or limitations stop you from getting the help that you need and deserve. Your future physical health and service connected benefits are sitting there waiting for you so go and get them!

What benefits am I talking about?

When talking about the VA I am not just talking about Service Connected financial payments. The VA has tons of things available to you:

- Medical – Eyes, Ears, Nose, and Throat. The whole body
- Dental
- Psychological
- Dermatological
- Podiatry
- Sleep Apnea
- In many cases free CPAP, Blood Pressure units & more
- Medications
- MRI's and X-rays
- And much more

Many of you can even qualify to receive travel pay for your visits. Now where else can you get that?

Many of the larger VA hospitals even have:

- Gyms and Workout Classes
- Water Therapy & Aerobics
- Library with free books
- Game and Meeting Rooms with Computers and Internet

This guide is not a government advertisement for the VA

I am not affiliated! I am a veteran just like you. I hid out from the VA for many years myself.

There are many thousands of veterans hiding themselves away all over the world. These vets are from WWII, Korea, Vietnam and now Iraq, and Afghanistan. They live dark unhealthy lives hidden inside and away from the things that make life worth living. They only come out into the light to get another bottle of booze or bag of drugs.

There are also many thousands of vets living lives as functioning alcoholics and drug users. They may carry on with their jobs but due to PTSD their family and social lives are rocky and they live in fear of having it all blow apart at any time.

Why do so many hide?

Unfortunately many vets did try to get help in the early days but did not find the help that they needed. There just wasn't the understanding and knowledge available in the medical community to give the proper diagnosis, information and therapy that now is available to you.

Another unfortunate problem that vets have run into is the incredible size of the Veterans Administration. It can be daunting and confusing. Much more so at first. Also like all institutions there are great employees and there are ones that aren't so easy to deal with.

PBAD's

There are two types of PBADs:

- Persons Behind a Desk - Someone who does their job well and is willing to be helpful.
- Prisoners' Behind a Desk – Someone who is not as happy with their job. This very well can be a temporary condition subject to the attitude of the previous veteran in the line you are standing in. Remember **"Vets Helping Vets!"** The person behind you in line will be forever grateful if you turn this particular PBAD from a Prisoner into a Person with a smiling face.

Usually these PBADs are the first people a vet comes into contact with at the VA. Some are paid employees and some are volunteers. Please treat the volunteers with the utmost respect. They choose to be there, for free, to help us.

Of course treat all PBADs with patience as their work can be difficult. If you are a vet then you know how interesting we all can be. We can be a grumpy bunch ☺

Now just being nice doesn't always work so do not let a PBADs attitude chase you into the hills. Before you run for the parking lot spend some time talking with the other vets that are there waiting on appointments or hanging around outside the VA waiting for a ride or just having a smoke. In most cases they will have a long background in dealing with the VA. This probably will end up being a "Bitch Session." We vets like to do that, but it should be oddly comforting. It reinforces the **"Vets Helping Vets"** thing and lets you know that you are not alone. Also you can learn a lot of important shortcuts as many of we older vets have been there and done that. Remember that the PBADs would not have a job if it wasn't for us. They do work for us! Do not let them steal your benefits by chasing you away.

Never, Never, Never
Give Up on your Recovery!

This is worth going over again

If you allow a bad experience, or even several bad experiences, at the VA stop you from getting the benefits, that are rightfully yours, you are not only hurting yourself but your family as well. Your benefits could include many great things depending on how well you learn to work within the system.

Depending on your situation it could include:

- Monthly Financial Help
- Medical and Psychological Checkups
- In-Depth Medical Testing
- MRI's
- Operations
- Medications
- Dental Work & much more....

Important Note:

Do not misunderstand what is being said in regard to the VA. Most Veterans go there and have no problems whatsoever. Unfortunately, you rarely hear anything about the good experiences. The vet is happy with the help he or she received and probably won't run up and down the street holding a big smiley face sign saying **"I Love the VA."** On the other hand the vets that do have a problem tend to yell loudly about their bad experience and then never go back.

The VA is at the forefront of PTSD Research due to the tremendous number of veterans they see on a daily basis. It is a huge mistake for a veteran to not take advantage of the big advancements being made in PTSD Research and therapy at the VA.

First Things First: Let's get specific

You are a veteran. Are you having issues that you can't get a handle on? Are you reacting to things in a way that you don't fully understand? As I have stated in the last chapter take the time to do a careful Self-Evaluation Test:

- What were you like before you went to war?
- Have your plans for what you wanted to do with your life radically changed?
- Do you get bored with mundane jobs and daily chores much quicker than in the past?
- Do small mistakes that people around you make cause you to never want to trust them again? Do you then want nothing more to do with them? Have you lost all trust for non-vets that were not in a War Zone with you?
- Do you go from calm to extreme in a red eyed flash?
- Do you have Road Rage?
- Do you dangerously over react to things that would not have bothered you before the war?
- Has your family and friends began to shy away from the different you that you have become?

These are just a few of the things that may not concern you by themselves but when added up start to cause you worry. "What is going on with me? Why am I doing things that are screwing up everything?"

These are unsettling negative questions. They really cause confusion and stress that leads to even more anger.

One of the many important things that are covered in this guide is ways to turn negative personal questions, like those above, into positive reinforcing ones.

Learning how to turn negative thoughts into positive ones is an important step toward becoming a Warzone PTSD Survivor

The Power of Positive Thinking is not just a cliché bandied about in seminars. It is a major tool for not just your mental health but it is a key tool to your physical health as well. (See Chapters 6 & 7)

Most psychiatrists believe that Post Traumatic Stress Disorder, keyword being Disorder, doesn't start to manifest itself as a disorder for at least a month after the event or events take place. In many cases it doesn't manifest itself for years. The sufferer may start becoming antsy and their anger becomes more noticeable over time. It is a progression so you and your family may not notice it creeping up until it becomes severe.

In my case I did not realize I had problems for many years. Unfortunately, this was much more common for my era of military service. With no acronym like PTSD to hang the strange behavior on, there was not much that the doctors could do. It was like, "Oh well. Here comes another one of those Vietnam vets needing more time to straighten out and re-adjust."

Today most soldiers coming back from a War Zone are well aware of the potential for these types of issues to crop up. Now everyone, especially in the military, has heard of PTSD!

Many soldiers hide their problems as they fear it will stall their return home at the end of their deployment. If they say anything they could be placed into therapy. It is unfortunate that being held over probably will happen to them so most returning soldiers learn to shove their problems under the rug. Stage #1 in the Hiding Out frame of mind!

PTSD Symptoms

Here are three common classes of symptoms that end in a diagnosis of PTSD. Most practitioners believe that you need to experience all three for a true diagnosis of PTSD. Remember there is PTS, which is stress, caused by an event. PTSD with the "D" becomes a **disorder** when someone continues to experience these issues over and over for a prolonged period of time:

- *Class 1 symptoms:* the sufferer re-experiences the traumatic incident – Some *examples: nightmares, flashbacks.*
- *Class 2 symptoms:* the sufferer displays avoidance, wants to stay away from anything that may possibly remind her/him of the trauma. They may also display lack of responsiveness or interest in all life circumstances. Not being willing to go out in

public or crowds is common.

Some examples of the things that cause them trouble: sights, smells, sounds, conversations associated or reminding of trauma, unable to enjoy once joyful activities or have loving feelings

- *Class 3 symptoms:* hyper-arousal / hyper-vigilance

Some examples- Fear of crowds, irritability, inability to sleep, sitting with your back to a wall in public places.

Hyper vigilance is one of the symptoms of PTSD and refers to the experience of being constantly tense and "on guard." A person experiencing this symptom of PTSD will be motivated to maintain an increased awareness of their surrounding environment, sometimes even frequently scanning the environment to identify potential sources of threat. Hyper vigilance is also often accompanied by changes in behavior, such as always choosing to sit in a far corner of a room so as to have awareness of all exits. At extreme levels, hyper vigilance may appear similar to paranoia.

Despite the fact that the above mentioned three classes of PTSD symptoms are most often present immediately after the traumatic incident, there are times when they show up much later, resulting in delayed-onset PTSD.

Below are Notes on the above Classes of symptoms:

Class 1 Symptoms:

Flashbacks are common but they don't always show up as actually believing you are back in the war. In my case they showed up as a photo type picture rather than a movie that would flash into my mind at odd times. It is shocking but I would try to shake it off.

I have talked to thousands of vets and have received hundreds of different types of ways these flashbacks can occur.

Most vets experience nightmares for a while and even years later. My wife told me about waking up with me grabbing her and shaking her or swinging wildly, etc. I started strangling her once in our sleep. I do not remember these things but believe me she remembers.

Class 2 Symptoms:

Avoidance is one of the biggest problems in becoming a PTSD Survivor. Hiding out from the terrible thoughts is the worst thing that a person can do. Shoving the thoughts down into a dark corner of the mind allows them to build and push the sufferer into all types of bad reactions to normal situations. The longer the avoidance stretches the deeper the trauma spreads roots that will disrupt a person's life.

Exposure Therapy can be a good tool to help with Avoidance Issues. We will discuss this more in this chapter.

Another instance of Class 2 symptoms that really bothered me was the lack of responsiveness and disconnection. For example when my favorite aunt died I felt nothing. This type of thing still happens today 45 years after I left a War Zone. It was hard to get my head around this.

I now understand why this happens. You can't take the time to feel sorrow for a dead buddy when you are under fire and fighting for your life. Stopping to mourn could very well be deadly to you. Even so it is unnerving when this disconnection continues to happen now. It is one of the things you learn to live with if you want to be a PTSD Survivor. Becoming a PTSD Survivor involves learning patience and understanding of your own quirks and anger issues that past traumas have caused you. As you learn some of the mental techniques explained in this Guide you will find that they **will** become second nature after a little practice. Once they begin to happen automatically you will be able to call yourself a War Zone PTSD Survivor.

Class 3 symptoms: hyper-arousal and hyper-vigilance

If you start to notice that some people will insist on sitting with their back to a wall you will get an example of hyper-arousal and you probably are looking at a vet or an Old West gunslinger☺.

In my case I kept moving further and further out into the high desert of California. You can see for miles. There are very few places for someone to hide and attack me. People started calling me Desert Don. I now live way north of the Antelope Valley of California on the road toward Death Valley. That is as far as we are going. Ginger will not deal well with me changing my name to: Death Valley Don!

Hyper-arousal can manifest itself in many ways such as road rage, anger issues and much more. Car backfires will point out any vets in the crowd. They are the ones on the ground!

Types of Therapy available at the VA:

- Exposure Therapy
- Drug Therapy
- Talk Therapy
- Cognitive-behavioral Therapy
- ACT – Acceptance and Commitment Therapy

- Behavioral Therapy
- Interpersonal Therapy
- Anger Management Therapy
- Marriage and Family Counseling

Exposure Therapy: Ten years ago I started going to meetings at a Vet Center. When I first was introduced to these meetings I didn't know what Exposure Therapy was or what purpose it served.

Note: The Vet Centers were established because many Vets were not comfortable with going to the Veterans Hospitals and asking for help. The VA reminded many of us of Big Brother. Even so I snuck out the door of the first three attempts I made to get help at the Vet Center in the San Fernando Valley.

I finally sat through my first meeting, which was a round table group BS session headed by a psychologist.

Note: Thanks go out to Dr Irving Borstein who ran my group. He was really awesome. During my time under his tutelage a vet he was interviewing got the idea that Dr Borstein was a Viet Cong interrogator. The guy jumped across the Doc's desk and started strangling him. Dr Borstein gained his own PTSD Issues☺. His job was not an easy one.

During my first meetings we all spent an hour telling war stories. I did not understand the purpose of this and it really made me nervous. The second I got out of the Vet Center meeting I ran to the nearest liquor store to help sooth my raw exposed nerve endings. Is that what was meant by Exposure Therapy? Pull out your bad memories and smash them with an entrenching tool!

This went on for a couple of months. After a time it no longer made me nervous to talk about my experiences and I didn't mind opening up about things that I never would have talked about before.

A simple explanation of Exposure Therapy is that it allows a person to talk about past traumas and break them up into bite sized bits so that the mind can demystify them and get them out into the open.

I still feel that I would have handled the meetings much better, in the first place, if I had been given a heads up on what to expect in Exposure Therapy. This is your heads up! Expect these feelings.

You will think that the sessions are not working and that you are getting worse. Let your wife and your friends know that you may experience these feelings as they will no doubt notice you acting more uptight after the meetings.

I personally feel that Exposure Therapy is a great way to get started on the road to recovery now that I understand what Exposure Therapy is. There are several types of Exposure Therapy available at the VA or Vet Centers. The important thing is to get into a group and try it out. Any of the groups is a start. If you will dig in you will find one that you are comfortable with and it is "Step One" in your living a better life.

Does that sound too easy and smack of happy horseshit? It is still the truth and it is a giant first step. It took me 40 years to finally dig in and seriously ask for help. Don't make that same mistake. If you have put it off and have been dealing with this as long as I have, don't worry, it is anything but too late. The programs didn't start helping me until I let my guard down and agreed that I had issues by finally doing a strong **Self Examination**.

Also I didn't get my 100% Service Connected Disability until I was 60. Getting financial benefits does take a huge load of pressure off! You will be pleasantly surprised at the other benefits you could be eligible for. That will be discussed in detail in the Chapter on VA Benefits.

Note to friends and relatives – These types of questions would not be considered Exposure Therapy

- Did you kill anyone?
- Did you wound any children?

- What was war like?
- Were you afraid of dying?
- In my case "What did it feel like getting shot in the butt?"

No one actually asked me that last one but you can't believe some of the questions I was asked especially back in the "Spit on a Vietnam Vet" Days. People actually called us things like "baby killers"!

I learned to make up things to get out of talking about it like: "That information is still classified and I would have to kill you if I talked to you." That would drive them crazy. It really piqued their curiosity but they were worried: "Would he really have to kill me?"☺

Drug Therapy

This is a tough one for me as I sit here writing this Guide. I am extremely anti-drugs for a number of reasons. Drugs messed up a large portion of not only my life but also many of my friends' lives as well. A number of my friends are no longer with us due to them.

Also the VA Hospitals, especially in the days right after Vietnam, handed out drugs like candy for everything from a hangnail to a headache. Many vets abused the VA for that reason. Some became drug dependent due to this.

In another book I used this acronym below for the early days of the VA's response to what they called Shell Shock, Soldiers Heart or Battle Fatigue which we now call **PTSD**:

Please

Take

Some

Drugs

I no longer have that opinion of the new VA. In fact I am no longer totally anti-drug therapy under *extreme* conditions.

NO, I AM NOT NOW IN ANY WAY, SHAPE OR FORM PRO-DRUGS!

Don't misunderstand any of this without a lot more information on just how toxic all drugs are. There is not one drug manufactured that is non-toxic. Your body is a healing machine. One of its most important functions is the elimination of toxins. Don't add to the fire! There will be much more on this in Chapter 6 on Physical Healing.

If your doctors tell you that you need drugs, especially for things like cholesterol, high blood pressure or for mental issues then pay attention to them. Just understand that it is not a life sentence for drug use. By becoming proactive in your own body and mind you can eliminate them. The VA will give you a blood pressure monitor if you have high BP. Use it. Lose some weight and you will be surprised at just how easy it is to get off of BP Meds.

That being said you will want to weigh all of your options about Drug Therapy. I will give some information here that I hope will help you make smart choices. Until you fully understand and live the type of life outlined in Chapter 7 – Physical Health, you may very well need some temporary Drug Therapy.

Here is a situation that happened within my own family: A relative very close to me began experiencing delusional thoughts that were totally out of character for her. It seemed like she was having nervous breakdowns.

After several hospital stays she was placed on certain medications that helped stabilize her condition.

I went with her several times to her doctor's appointments. One thing I noticed at the psychiatrist's office that bothered me was the total lack of "Talk Therapy." The only questions she was asked were questions like: "How did that last prescription seem to work for you?" That was pretty much it!

Editor's Note: Talk Therapy will be discussed more in this chapter

She seemed better for about eight months until she stopped taking her medications as regularly as she had been. She seemed fine for some time and we hoped that she was going to be OK without drugs.

The psychiatrists did not talk to her about healthy alternatives that could help such as diet and exercise.

Through my research and studies of PTSD and other mental issues I hoped that Talk Therapy alone would now help her maintain her balance.

After about a month she again started having invasive thoughts and confusion. She went back into the hospital. I soon realized that no amount of Talk Therapy would get through to her while she was in this state.

Through more research and talking with psychiatrists and psychologists that I know I came to realize that the strength of the chemical changes in her brain would not allow her to fully understand what was going on in a way that talk therapy alone would be of help to her.

She was placed back on milder medications and in a reasonable period of time she was able to then get benefits from Talk Therapy.

What the doctors didn't tell me, because most of them don't know anything about prevention through physical hygiene and holistic health, was that the chemical changes in her body and brain were caused by her sketchy diet, lack of exercise and other bad habits that caused a buildup of toxins in her body.

Through proper exercise and a healthy regimen of good eating habits and food based quality vitamins and minerals she no longer has any need for drugs. She no longer has chemical imbalances in the brain.

Note: A *nervous breakdown* refers to a mainstream and often-used term to generically describe someone who experiences a bout of mental illness that is so severe, it directly impacts their ability to function in everyday life. The specific mental illness can be anything — depression, anxiety, bipolar disorder, schizophrenia, or something else. But the reference to a "nervous breakdown" usually refers to the fact that the person has basically stopped their daily routines — going to work, interacting with loved ones or friends, even just getting out of bed to eat or shower.

A nervous breakdown can be seen as a sign that one's ability to cope with life or a mental illness has been overwhelmed by stress, life events, and work or relationship issues. By disconnecting from their regular responsibilities and routines, an individual's nervous breakdown may allow them to try and regroup their coping skills and temporarily relieve the stress in their life.

Before this I felt that Talk Therapy alone was the glue to a balanced life. I learned a lot from this family situation and now understand the need, in some extreme situations, for temporary Drug Therapy. I still feel that Drug Therapy should be looked at as a temporary Band-Aid until the issue of good health is resolved and takes over. In the case of PTSD it must be followed with extended Talk Therapy, Anger Management and other forms of help. These are the long term tools that will last a lifetime.

Drug Therapy by itself has a large potential for a return to the basic problems once the Band-Aid of drugs is removed. Without looking at good physical health the drugs will continue to make matters in the physical body worse in other areas. The sufferer will then need more drugs. I am sure you know people who take upwards of 10 drugs per day. The physical damage caused by this doctor prescribed poison soup is beyond belief.

Keep in mind that I am writing this guide in relation to PTSD. If someone has been in a car crash and needs major surgery no amount of healthy living will stop the need for temporary pain relief and other drugs. However, the healthy person will recover at an extremely advanced rate.

This is where health comes into play; some people that experience conditions such as Bipolar Disorder may need to take one or two (not 10) medications for the rest of their lives to live a stable life. This is because many with bipolar issues won't stay on track with health and exercise. Their condition causes them to live a sporadic type of life with massive highs and lows.

I still believe that if they lived a healthy lifestyle of good eating, sleeping, etc. they wouldn't need drugs. Someone susceptible to things like Bipolar Disorder must be vigilant with their health regimen. With a history of erratic mood swings they must not let their blood sugars and other physical mood reactors run rampant. This can definitely be controlled by diet, proper sleep, supplements and exercise.

Some veterans may be so traumatized by their War Zone experiences that they cannot go out in public, sleep at night or any number of other problems. The lack of sleep, self-medication and poor eating will exacerbate the problems. These vets may temporarily need certain medications to function.

Note: I am not recommending the use of drugs of any type. This is a subject that must be discussed between you and your Doctor. Keep in mind though that most doctors don't look at drugs from a position of long term prevention. They only understand the fast fix or instant gratification scenario.

The information in this chapter is strictly added to give you some food for thought. By that I mean healthy food!☺

Talk Therapy

In order to heal we have to break the silence. With the right therapist, psychotherapy gives us tools for learning how to do that.

Talk Therapy is something I can go on and on about. That is probably because I never shut up! Unfortunately, too many psychiatric doctors are being forced to shut up!

Here is an example of that. Draw your own conclusions. I am not going to draw any conclusions from this myself in print (Legal Statement). Also a **Rant Alert** would be appropriate here as well.

In one hour a psychiatrist can probably write ten or more prescriptions for drugs. In that same hour of one on one Talk Therapy a psychiatrist may have time to see only two or three patients max.

If you were making recommendations to the doctor from the drug Industry or insurance company's point of view which scenario would you push for. Key word being **Push**! Hey I left the ER off the end of that word. Now that is a play on words indeed. ER or Emergency Room is what you may need after all the drugs they want to push at you. I guess it doesn't take a lot of insight to see where my feelings lay with regard to the drug and insurance companies.

Wow that actually felt good! What a Rant! Sorry everyone but when you really look at the over use of drugs in the medical community you should be as upset as I am along with many of my friends and associates as well.

Great Talk Therapy News for Vets

Now here is some really good news for veterans. The VA has many Talk Therapy Programs for you to benefit from. Not only are they good, they are also free to most veterans! In many situations you can even receive travel pay to attend these sessions!

Some vets under 30% Service Connected Benefits may have a small co-pay on the meetings depending on their income. Do not let that stop you. If the meetings lead to you receiving Service Connected Benefits it is worth it.

Note: More on Co-Pay and Travel Pay in Chapter 5 on VA Benefits.

So what is talk therapy?

Talk type therapy can be as simple as talking with other vets about what is bothering you. To be considered therapy it should be done with a clinician. It can be helpful to talk to a friend as well. Your friend may not have the answers that you need so finding the right group or Therapist is important.

Talking about your problems can help you spot things that are causing PTSD issues in your life. Getting someone's trained perspective on your problems can give you insight into ways to deal with them in a better way. Choose carefully who you talk to. Talking to vets or doctors at the VA is good. Talking everything out with your boss on the other hand may be tricky. I am not saying to not talk to people you work with, just be very selective.

Having a qualified therapist as a sounding board can save a lot of time. They will have training and have studied experiences that can help you see things that don't seem obvious to you.

There are a number of types of therapies that could fall into the category of Talk Therapy. We could even call Exposure Therapy, which was discussed above, as a form of this. There are differences in them but they all will be helpful.

First I'll give you some basic info on Talk Therapy. Later in this chapter I will identify, by name, some great programs available at many VA Hospitals and Vet Centers.

Here are several basic types of Talk Therapy?

Cognitive Behavioral Therapy

(CBT) can help you change harmful ways of thinking. If you tend to look at things too negatively you can learn to see things in a better light. With practice you can make this change more automatic. People around you will see this in a hurry, which will reinforce positive behavior in you. You will need to trust that this can happen. That actually would be a step in thinking more positive thoughts. Positive thinking is like building up your biceps. The more you exercise the easier it gets.

Example: You stop by to talk to a friend but she is in a hurry and doesn't have time to talk to you right now. Negative thinking would cause you to worry that she doesn't like you or is angry with you. This can lead to a flood of negative thoughts.

Therapy: With good positive cognitive tools you can be more understanding and appreciate that your friend is actually busy. You will understand that this is a busy world and you can talk to your friend latter. Thinking of other reasons for her actions will help you see the event in a more positive and accurate way.

ACT- Acceptance & Commitment Therapy

From the "third generation" of behavior therapies, ACT is a contextual approach challenging clients to accept their thoughts and feelings and still commit to change.

Client: "*I want to change, BUT I am too anxious.*"

Social worker: "*You want to change, AND you ARE anxious about it.*"

This subtle verbal and cognitive shift is the essence of acceptance and commitment therapy (ACT). It suggests that a person can take action without first changing or eliminating feelings. Rather than fighting the feeling attached to a behavior, a person can observe oneself as having the feeling but still act. Acceptance-based approaches postulate that instead of opting for change alone, the most effective approach may be to accept and change. The importance of acceptance has long been recognized in the Serenity Prayer at AA meetings.

As one of the postmodern behavioral approaches, ACT is being evaluated as another short-term intervention in a variety of populations seen by social workers.

Behavioral Therapy will help you get over behavior that is causing you problems. If a certain type of behavior continues to give you a bad result, such as being late all the time, you can't expect that it will all of a sudden be OK to be late.

This requires you learning certain tools to adjust your timing. The goal is to get control over behavior that is causing problems for you.

These are simple things when looked at from the outside. Behavioral Therapy will help you internalize them so that they become good habits. Changing bad habits for good ones isn't hard once you start to make a commitment to living a better life.

Interpersonal therapy helps you get along with others. You'll focus on how to express your feelings, and how to develop better people skills. It will also help you reach out in a positive way to ask for help. Asking for help is something vets don't readily like to do.

Examples: You and your mother are not getting along. She doesn't approve of your significant other, or your group of friends. You feel that she is trying to run your life.

Therapy: Talk therapy can help you see your mother's point of view. Perhaps she feels you don't spend time with her anymore. Finding new ways of talking to your mother helps you both feel better.

Remember that talk therapy doesn't have to be difficult. The simple act of discussing your feelings allows you to gain new insight and perspective. Talk therapy can also help to enrich your life by bringing the people that you love closer to you.

Another example: Year after year you refuse to speak to your wife about the bad thoughts you deal with from the war. Because you two don't talk about it you begin to feel she doesn't care. After so much time she may be afraid to bring up those subjects and she just lives with your problems.

This can develop into your wife developing her own version of PTSD.

Therapy: By talking to her a little at a time about the problems you are dealing with you will become a team that can help each other make your lives better together. Keeping it bottled up is a sure fire prescription for causing larger problems.

Anger Management Therapy

Anger is one of the biggest problems that a person with PTSD must face. Anger is extremely common with the condition.

Anger is a natural emotion that every human and many non-human animals experience. Mild forms of human anger may include displeasure, irritation or dislike. When we react to frustration, criticism or a threat, we may become angry - and usually this is a healthy response. Anger may be a secondary response to feeling sad, lonely or frightened. When anger becomes a full-blown rage our judgment and thinking can become impaired and we are more likely to do and say unreasonable and irrational things.

Anger is not just a mental state of mind. It triggers an increase in heart rate, blood pressure and levels of adrenaline and noradrenalin. Anger has survival benefits, and forms part of our *fight or flight* brain response to a perceived threat of harm. When a human or animal decides to take action to stop or confront a threat, anger usually becomes the predominant feeling and takes over our behavior, cognition and physiology.

In many cases humans and non-human animals express anger by making loud sounds, baring teeth, staring and specific posturing as a warning to perceived aggressors to stop their threatening behaviors. It is unusual for a physical attack to occur without these signs of anger appearing first. If a stranger approaches some newborn puppy-dogs the mother will most likely growl, bare her teeth and adopt a defensive or ready-to-attack posture, rather than silently attack without any warning.

If you trespass into the private land of a farmer in a remote area, his approach may be similar; his voice may be hostile, as may his body language, and posture. Instinctively, anger may surge in humans and non-human animals to protect territory, offspring and family members, secure mating privileges, prevent loss of possessions or food, and many other perceived threats.

Experts say anger is a primary, natural emotion with functional survival value, which we all experience from time to time. The raised heart rate, blood pressure, and release of hormones prepare us physically for remedial action - which is either to fight or run away at top speed (fight or flight).

The fight or flight issue is raised to a new level for warriors. Unfortunately, in peace time it rolls over into nasty things like Road Rage and a super short fuse when dealing with issues at home and work.

Many VA Hospitals have programs dealing with Anger Management. It is important that you get involved with a support group or talk to your doctor about it and find out what your options are to deal with it.

There are a number of tools that I have learned to use in dealing with my anger. A good healthy fear of anger is one. I am lucky to be alive due to the number of times my anger has put me in front of someone with a gun or a knife.

Also, Road Rage has placed my wife and kids in harm's way and has caused them way too much stress and fear because of my road monitoring urges.

No matter how often I flipped someone the finger or shook my head at them there was always some other idiot driver to rapidly take their place. You can't get rid of them all. All you can do is turn them into enemies that want to run you off the road or worse.

I have taught myself to spot bad or rude drivers way back in my rear view mirror. I automatically start to change lanes so that I don't have to deal with them.

In the old days I would look forward to spotting them in my rear view so that I could tap the breaks or slow way down when they crawled up my rear end. I treated it like a video game. The trouble is that this particular video game can become extremely deadly not to mention what it does to your blood pressure.

Stopping this bad behavior becomes easier the more you do it. Dangerous behavior takes a little practice to change but it is well worth it. Teaching yourself to leave a little earlier is a great tool to use in combating Road Rage as long as you keep reminding yourself that you are early. Even being early won't stop a bad habit like road rage. You have to turn it into a good habit by reminding yourself "I am early. I don't need to speed." I don't need to flip that person off!

Good Tool: I like to place pictures of my grandkids on the dashboard. This has an extremely good grounding effect on me. Use something that has a calming effect on you. Make it something that you want to live longer for like your family and friends. If you don't have family or friends it could be a sign that you really could use Anger Management!

Anger Management Therapy will teach you many mental tools to add to your arsenal. Also talking with other vets about their anger problems will help you see how dangerous those problems are. In many cases it allows you to see how dumb most of the things that upset you really are. Seeing it come from someone else points out the absurdity of it.

In anger Management Groups there is usually some laughter but it is accompanied by red faces because when you hear someone else's dumb story about a boneheaded anger issue it usually hits way too close to home.

Anger Issues go hand in hand with PTSD and they will ruin your relationships with loved ones, friends and people in the work place! Get proactive with Anger Management as soon as possible. You will hear the term **Proactive** in this guide a number of times. If you won't get fully involved with your recovery it just will not happen.

Your PTSD Issues will not go away by themselves.

Get Started:

Contact your local VA today!

Red Flags in Anger Management

Usually rage or anger of any kind takes a little time to develop. Look at it like climbing a slope with red flags spaced evenly along the climb. The lower down the slope you teach yourself to spot those red flags the sooner you can train yourself to ratchet down the severity of the problem. If you keep turning a blind eye to the flags you won't be able to control the outcome.

With practice you will actually spot these red flags much quicker. How much time does it take? Not that long at all if you do it with intention!

There are studies on this but all I can speak from is my own personal experiences. With intention and repetition it gets easier and easier. The end result is worth every bit of effort you can give it. Do you ever totally rid yourself of this behavior? I am not sure as I am still a work in progress myself. I am not perfect and never will be. I am much better than I used to be. My wife likes going on drives with me now. I enjoy it much more myself. With practice I have learned to enjoy the moment so to speak. I no longer feel like I am in a hurry to get to the next thing.

You have to consciously intend to change. Living with intention to change and attention to your bad habits takes more work at first but gets much easier over time.

That is why I still go to a weekly PTSD and Substance Abuse program. I am a creature of habit. I need the weekly reminders or I will slip back into, as my wife likes to call it, The Bad Old Days!

Marriage and Family Counseling

PTSD and Substance Abuse in most cases are co-occurring (Co-morbid) conditions. They cause major problems within the family and flow over into friendships as well! Many veterans have had numerous spouses and/or relationships.

These huge problems affect everyone in the family and all those close to the Vet. Can you imagine the problems that occur with husbands and wives that have both been in a War Zone? Talk about PTSD Squared!

A powerful problem that is usually overlooked is what happens to the long-term spouse of a Veteran with PTSD. Having PTSD by contact is extremely traumatic. The spouses are usually overlooked and spend years in the background as a caregiver and more often a dart board for everything that goes wrong.

The spouse holds everything in while helping as their husband or wife deal with their more obvious red flag problems. This can build over the years with unexpected strength until the spouse explodes.

This can easily cause divorce, nervous breakdowns or in really bad situations violent confrontations.

Marriage and Family Counseling should be looked at as soon as someone realizes they have PTSD Issues. People with PTSD can easily become consumed with their own problems and overlook what it is doing to everyone else around them until it is too late.

First Steps to the "What's Next" Question!

1. Take a good hard look at yourself. Do a **Self-Evaluation Test** as spoken about above. Realize that you have a problem that could be PTSD and "Just Do Something!" Reading this guide or starting to do research on your own is a good first step. **Do not hide!** The Internet has tons of good info but don't let it slow you down. Months of private research is months that you could also have spent talking to other Vets at places like the

Veterans Hospital or Vet Centers. Do Not Hide! That is worth saying over and over again!

2.   Once at the VA or Vet Center - Talk! Ask Questions. Ask about getting into a PTSD program. This will help you get started talking about the things you have been shoving down into your Hidey Hole. Until you break down the barrier of talking about what is bothering you, you will remain stuck in that dark cave!

3.   Don't run and hide! Do not let a PBAD (Prisoner Behind a Desk) or bad experience at a VA rob you of your benefits. I will go over this much more in Chapter #5 on VA Benefits.

Now all this is much easier than you thought, right? That's coming from the guy who snuck out of my first two attempts at talking to someone at the Vet Center. Many worthwhile things in life are not easy on the surface but as you dig in you will find that it was not nearly as hard as you had built it up to be. The most important thing that I ever did was to go back for the third time and that time I stayed!

You must do these first steps. Don't even think about it. Just do it! Yes it is out of your comfort zone but how much good has that comfort zone done for you to date?

Important! The VA is much better than it used to be and getting better every day. If you want to get help and benefits then you will have to learn the steps involved. The VA is a learning curve. A learning curve always involves the first step forward. I will keep working to make it easier for you to take the first steps. Just ask me your questions on our message boards at:
WWW.PTSDHotline.Com

Here is the address of the Message Boards:
http://www.ptsdhotline.com/forum/forum.php

This website is there to back up this Guide and it is free, so use it!

Chapter 4

My Personal Recovery

My personal Recovery experiences

As I have said a few times in this guide this isn't about me! I am already living well and have control over the PTSD Issues that plagued me for years. This guide is about helping veterans who are still getting beat over the head with what war has caused them.

With that in mind I have decided to summarize my progression through my own PTSD story.

Actually I am one of you so my personal wicked winding road toward recovery will point out some of the nastier stumbling blocks and jagged pitfalls along the way so that you can avoid them.

The sooner you can learn the important steps to recovery the shorter your own journey will become.

Much of this below is a rehash of what I have already laid down in the previous chapters of this guide. I will attempt to put my experiences into the order that my personal recovery took.

This chronology is from 1963 to the present. That is how long it took me to recover from war. If you follow the steps in the last chapter of this guide you will reduce the time frame from years to months. That's including receiving Service Connected Benefits as well if you qualify! Of course the time frame depends on your willingness to become **Proactive!** It depends on how much time you are willing to devote to your own personal healing process?

1963 to 1966: After high school and before Vietnam I really enjoyed working at teamwork type situations in large companies. It made me feel good to be part of something big. I enjoyed working with others in a teamwork way.

After high school I worked in a huge glassworks factory that was like something out of Dante's Inferno. It was dark in the large dungeon like glass forming rooms. This put a real Hollywood spin on the molten blobs of glowing glass being lifted through the air in the pincher fingers of robotic arms. Everywhere you looked there were conveyer belts flying along at breakneck speeds. It was really exciting in a red-hot Hollywood sort of way. Things held a lot of wonder for me in my days before I went to war.

Next I worked as a Design Engineer for a large machine shop that was doing hydraulic and pneumatic systems for Bell Helicopter and others. Working on combat helicopters was as close to the Vietnam War as I was **hoping** to get.

1966 to 1968: Military Duty and the Vietnam War. So much for **hoping!**

1969 After Vietnam – Welcome Home! Back to "normal": To use the word normal relating to a returning warrior should be illegal in its overall stupidity!

My first job was in engineering for NBC's Cable TV Network. Good pay. Prestige. It should have been a really good experience.

Why then after two years did it feel so stifling? Before Vietnam this would have been my dream job! Why did I quit?

1972: Next job a large grocery warehouse:

Wow Excitement! Guys flying everywhere on powered carts towing small trailers loading semi-trucks full of cases of everything from soup to beer. Bosses and foremen sneaking us mini bennies (Amphetamine) to work us like madmen. Adrenaline, good pay, drugs, beer, thrills!

Why then did I jump across the Plant Superintendent's desk and start strangling him?

Was the job not exciting enough on its own? I guess not. I quit yet again!

1974 to Whenever! What a blur! The underground years!

Looking back on those years it is hard to put the 1970s into any type of perspective! A hippie with a hand grenade? Flower power with a machete?

- Down with the establishment!
- To hell with conformity!
- Rebel against Society!
- *Dr. Timothy Leary for President!

*Leary's most famous quote: "Turn on, Tune in, Drop out" must have been written for me!

What happened to college, engineering and being involved in large group type efforts that I used to love? I guess having another large group type effort (NVA/Vietcong) shooting back at me kind of soured the whole concept!

Forget big companies! Give me more excitement! I want to be a smuggler! I want to be a collection agent of sorts. I want to hang out with pirates!

After I came back from war I was a completely changed person who could not take orders or direction from anyone. I was extremely restless and became bored easily. I tried many different things to make a living. Many of the things I did were dangerous and most of them were underground activities. I was angry about everything and thought that the government did whatever it wanted to do and so could I. I could care less about what people thought of as normal.

I smoked a lot of pot, which I had learned to use in Vietnam. I saw very little drug use around in my earlier years. None of my friends used any before I went overseas and neither did I. After Nam there wasn't a drug I wouldn't smoke, swallow, or snort.

The alcohol and substance abuse was fueled by my need to forget the things that kept me up at night and also to fire my addiction to adrenaline! *In a War Zone adrenaline is your friend!*

My disruptive behavior got worse year by year. I needed more excitement to fulfill the void that "Normal Life" left in me.

I did not understand the changes in me and didn't really care as long as I could get the excitement I craved. I gravitated toward a whole different group of people and needed to constantly push the boundaries of acceptable behavior.

My wife and I fought a lot especially after we started having kids. My wild lifestyle was no place to raise our two daughters. I did everything outside the establishment. That did not bother me a bit because I felt that it was the establishment that had thrown me away as just another body bag for their money machine.

Actually, I still believe that. It is still going on full tilt today. I would go to war to fight a Hitler but the rest of it is beyond my understanding. Maybe I am just naive but I believe there are much better ways to take care of the Bin Laden's of the world without filling thousands more body bags and making candidates for PTSD.

Even though I still feel this way I had to stop letting it destroy my life and the people's lives around me. It really got to a point of sink or swim.

1977 The VA

My first attempts at dealing with the VA were waving my middle finger at it as I drove by. I drove to the general vicinity to appease

Ginger. She thought I was actually stopping in. I still didn't really believe I had a problem. I liked my wild and crazy lifestyle.

During this time I did put in for benefits for scars on my butt and arm. I received 15%.

1987 The Nightmare Years!

Aside from the War Zone nightmares and flashbacks I started having many long nights worrying about things like jail, the IRS and being bothered by the, "What the hell do I think I am doing" type of questions. I still didn't know how to ask myself positive questions.

I finally decided to try and rejoin society. I re-opened a family landscaping business that I had been involved with in my early years.

This was a huge change but not a complete break. That took much more time as I did not have the psychological tools available to me that I have today. I was willing to work hard and decided after a while that I kind of liked working with my hands and back. Designing beautiful landscapes was rewarding as long as I could just keep those damn customers and clients out of the picture.

I liked working for myself as there was no way I could have taken orders from anyone else. It was hard enough explaining to the clients that they didn't know crap about landscaping! Having to try to explain this to your boss would have caused even more problems. Did I have anger issues? Ask my clients from those days! The only thing that saved me was that I was actually pretty good at the job.

As is normal in the recovery process I had many downward spiral type setbacks during those years.

The next ten years were not an easy transition as I still had major anger issues that caused me to argue with my employees, customers and my internal battle that bubbled just below the surface of my pasted on smile.

Another interesting direction I took early in the late 1980s and1990s was my discovery of the Internet. Talk about a perfect playground for an ADD/PTSD madman.

I started an online sport fishing magazine. It had message boards☺. You cannot believe the madhouse those message boards became after cocktail hour. Oh wait, you are vets with PTSD. You can easily imagine the chaos. After all, I didn't have self-medication problems. I was just one more crazy fisherman yelling and lying about the size of my fish over one cocktail or was it ten!

1995: My sport fishing message boards had readership from all over the world. I could flip people off globally. This extra excitement went on well past my 50th birthday.

I started realizing that I hadn't changed anything. Yes, I was now living a legal lifestyle. Had I changed? Hell no! I was still self-medicating, yelling and screaming and acting nutty on the freeways.

Ginger and I were still fighting. We just were fighting about different things.

She convinced me to get more serious about finding help at the VA. I still had never heard of PTSD.

1997: I started going to the VA and asking questions like, "Why am I doing all these stupid things?" They scratched their heads and said, "Let's talk about it some more. How did that last drug work for you?" Just what I needed, More drugs! The VA still didn't have the great Talk Therapy Programs that they now have.

Even though the term PTSD had been whispered in some areas since the 1980s, I never personally heard of it at the VA until after 2000.

I went ahead and put in a new Benefits Claim asking for help because I was fighting with my landscape customers, my sport fishing Internet community and anyone who got in my way on the freeways.

It was causing me to barely make a living and led to real struggles with my family and friends as well.

The VA did boost my benefits from 15% to 60%. They said, "OK let's talk about your problems some more," with that same bewildered look on their faces.

After some of their head scratching sessions I stopped going back as it wasn't doing me any good other than a little extra money per month which I did appreciate. I lived a long way from the VA and I didn't know about Travel Pay. Funny, no one working at the VA mentioned Travel Pay until a fellow veteran brought it up a few years later. That is Vets Helping Vets in a big way!

I didn't understand the term **Becoming Proactive** until later. That was to my detriment. That is why I bring up becoming proactive so many times in this guide! It can really affect your life and pocketbook!

2003: The term Post Traumatic Stress Disorder started popping up on the news as it related to a War Zone. I no longer did drugs or smoked pot. I had given that all up in the 1990s. I was still having serious problems with my favorite red wine though. I didn't drink it. I inhaled it.

In part that was due to my drug days. Most drugs grabbed you fast and hard. If I did something I wanted instant gratification. Why would anyone want to sip at anything? I did the same thing in the earlier days with things like Jack Daniels. Wham Bam and down the gullet it went. I tried to calm that down by becoming a wino instead. Fifths switched to Gallons!

Ginger and I talked (argued) a lot about giving the VA another shot. I didn't feel confident about the VA so I took a stab at trying the Vet Centers. As I have mentioned in an earlier chapter my first couple of attempts at this ended in me sneaking out the back door.

I finally met with a PBAD (a good one) there and he convinced me to sit in on a meeting. It was better than I expected. I started attending round table sessions. I liked the other vets there right away. After a time these meetings felt good and I went to them for over a year. People close to me started noticing small changes in me for the better. We had a great guy running the group - Dr. Irving Borstein, Ph.D.. Unfortunately, he retired from the VA and our group was disbanded. The Vet Centers do things like this once in a while. There was no follow up by them to see how any of us were doing.

Because of this I got upset and stopped going back to the Vet Center. I still didn't grasp the proactive thing. If I had I would have immediately found another group. Vets don't like change so I hid out for another year.

I slowly started reverting to my old ways. Because of some of the things I had learned at my meetings I did not like the reverse changes I saw happening again to me. I couldn't work as I wanted to strangle all my customers. I didn't actually want to kill anyone with my hands, but the thought of jumping out from behind one of the trees that I was installing and scaring a client to death gave me a real giddy high.

I quit trying to work with my back but wasn't making a good enough living arguing with fishermen after cocktail hour to cover everything. I put the sport fishing site up for sale.

2005: Luckily, I started hearing about a new weekly Program at the VA called the **PTSD and Substance Abuse Program.** I told Ginger I would go in and check it out. I couldn't believe it took the VA this long to realize the correlation between PTSD and Substance Abuse. By then I knew enough to know I needed in depth help so I dug in. Yes I finally became **Proactive!**

The program used a large workbook entitled "Seeking Safety" by Harvard Doctor Lisa Nejavits. It is broken down into many segments and we covered another segment each week.

I soon realized that this was like a graduate course in PTSD recovery. We did not sit around telling war stories like the other programs I had been involved in. We were asked not to bring war stories up as they worked against the training we were receiving. This was all about finding what was safe for us to maintain equilibrium in life.

Having gone through Exposure Therapy helped me appreciate this more cerebral approach. I would not have gotten as much out of it if I hadn't broken down my barriers in the earlier program.

What also helped me was that because it was at the VA and not the Vet Center I could receive travel pay to help me get there. This was important as I lived 100 miles from the Sepulveda VA.

Here are a few of the important weekly topics that are covered in this program:

- Grounding Techniques
- Watching for Red Flags
- Triggers
- Coping Skills
- Disconnecting from people
- Asking for help in the right places
- Creating Meaning
- Setting Boundaries
- When Substances control you
- Self-Nurturing
- Honesty
- And much more.........

I could give you tons of info and tools in this Guide. This would be counterproductive! Just reading a list here is not the same as getting you into a program like this at the VA. You need the interaction with the doctors and more importantly making connections with other vets who are going through the same things that you are. This interaction is a major tool in your recovery.

There are hundreds of books out there with all types of ideas on your recovery. If just reading them would have given you your life back then why haven't you done it? The key is the active interaction with your fellow vets!

2006: After being involved in the program for a while some other vets that I got to know convinced me to put in a new claim for the PTSD problems I was living with. I put in another claim.

After meeting with doctors inside and outside the VA I was raised to 80% with 100% unemployable status. I guess they didn't want me jumping out of trees on top of anyone's head. Keep that gorilla out of the banana trees!

2007 to Present: Getting 100% status was huge. It has given me a ton of benefits, which I will go over in **Chapter #5 VA Benefits.**

During this time Ginger and I also received our SSI (Social Security). This has allowed us to donate all our time to building websites to help other veterans and to write books like this guide.

Do I still have issues? You bet I do. I still like wine. I just choose not to drink a ton of it! Thanks to the PTSD and Substance Abuse/Seeking Safety Program I have gained tools to stop me from a downward spiral when one raises its ugly head.

Do I still have Road Rage? Yep to that too! It tries to sneak in every so often but I beat it back with thoughts of my grandkids. Having their photos in my vehicle really helps with that. These are simple tools that work for me! You will find your own with a little practice.

More complex times

Was living in a War Zone tough? Yes, but it was also really simple. You knew where the boundaries were and what to do next. You knew who to trust. You had your brothers in arms! You were given uniforms, food and told what to do next.

Living with PTSD after your service years is the diabolical one. All of a sudden you have to make so many choices for yourself. First you have to find out the hard way that you even have this thing called PTSD. It is incredibly tricky. A little booze or drugs will quiet it right back down, won't it? Well maybe at first anyway!

How many times did you think about re-enlisting? Going back to the War Zone might be easier? It is really confusing out here! Life was a lot simpler over there.

Coming home for good takes some real work: **deprogramming/reprogramming**.

The most important things that you can learn are:

- **You Are Not Alone!**
- **Just Do Something – Get started**
- **Become Proactive in your recovery!**
- **Never, Never, Never give up on your recovery**

We now know what PTSD is and we can beat it. What took me 40+ years you can do in months now that the monster is out of the closet!

Tom's Story

I have a good friend that is living with just half a lung still working due to Agent Orange. He was wounded being one of the first Marines into Vietnam. The day he was wounded his medic pulled a large chunk of shrapnel from his leg and patched him up. That day his medic and his superior officer in charge were both KIA. Because of this he did not receive his Purple Heart. On top of that he is a poster boy for PTSD.

Over the years he became furious with the VA because he was turned down for benefits over and over again, even though he had to carry an oxygen tank wherever he goes. He couldn't get benefits for Agent Orange because he didn't have diabetes to go along with his lung problems. That's just another Catch 22 at the VA. He didn't get benefits for PTSD either because they didn't understand it like they do now. He kept getting shafted by all the "Catch 22's" that can crop up while dealing with the VA.

He gave up until he and I met a year ago. He is now back in the system and taking important steps like going to PTSD Programs at the VA and working with the Purple Heart Association. Hopefully, he will now receive his benefits and will more than likely receive his Purple Heart. More importantly he is receiving quality help in his struggle with PTSD.

Authors Note: Good news on Tom's story in Chapter 5

Let's all say this together: Never, Never, Never Give Up On Your Recovery!

We must remember that the VA is there for the vets. You need to find out how to work within its system because it will impact your life in so many positive ways. Yes the VA can also tick you off but don't let that stop you!

Always stay connected to other vets. I will keep adding good info to this guide via our website. You can ask questions and get answers through the Message Boards:

WWW.PTSDHotline.Com

This is not just a hotline with a list of emergency contact info. There are a number of interesting sections containing tons of info that will help you make the right decisions regarding your future. Interactive message boards will be a powerful tool for you to use.

The next Chapter deals with **VA Benefits**. Important stuff!

Chapter 5
VA Benefits

In this chapter I will give you the step by step approach that I used to receive my benefits. I am at 100% overall.

Falling Through the Cracks!

Let's start off with an attempt to understand the gulf of misunderstandings that stands between some Veterans and the Veterans Administration.

Over the years I have talked with thousands of vets. Many have walked away from the VA in frustration and anger, never to return.

Simple economics and the incredible volume of returning veterans have caused a "Them Against Us" mentality to build.

It is not just the VA. For example what is the first thing that comes to your mind when you think of a visit to the Dept. of Motor Vehicles? Most people cringe even though Motor Vehicles have become much better!

It is the same with the VA. The VA is so much better than it was when the Vietnam Vets came home but due to the overwhelming overload of veterans it is easy to see why many vets come to feel neglected.

Here is a **hypothetical** situation:
This is not a true story! Legal Statement

There once was a country that sent its young people off to wars. In the beginning some of these wars were justified.

To deal with the thousands of returning (no longer young) war torn soldiers the country built an institution.

The country continued to wage wars that appeared to have less and less meaning. (Sorry I had to put this personal statement into this fictional story).

The institution ran into an escalating problem caused by the continuing list of wars, conflicts, etc. The institution was expected to keep up with the rapidly growing number of men and women who not only had mental and physical problems but needed financial help as well.

The institution found itself in an untenable situation in that if it helped every single returning soldier who needed physical, mental, and financial help it would implode. The institution had to survive at all **costs** (Pardon the intended pun).

Cracks in the system began to form. Many soldiers fell through these ever widening cracks. Due to this an interesting Catch 22 began to take place.

Soldiers who fell through the cracks did not receive mental, physical or financial help. The institution did not need to spend its funds on the soldiers who got upset and ran for the hills never to return.

- Did the institution realize this and set up a Crack Activation Department? No!
- Did the Institution set up a Crack Repair Department? Not to my knowledge!

This tug of war over the cracks caused a dysfunctional relationship to build between the institution and the returning soldiers. This was an extremely unfortunate situation as the institution did want to help as many as possible. **End of Fictional Story!**

Jumping All Cracks Trypophobia - Fear of holes, clusters, and **cracks!**
In this instance a little fear can be a really good thing.

Don't become a crack statistic! That sounds like a drug issue and it can be just as problematic to you in the long run.

This guide will give you the information that you need to avoid the cracks in the system. Just understanding this situation exists will help you make smarter choices. It's like playing one of those video games. The vets who end up with benefits learn how to jump over the problems. Information will get you part of the way. A desire to never give up and to take back your life will get you the rest of the way.

Receiving the benefits that you are entitled to will become a reality once you have a map to guide you around the cracks.

Important! Never take no for a final answer from the VA. The word "No" is just another one of those cracks. Jump it! Every Vet who has used this advice has ended up receiving help in one form or another that can include:

- Monthly Financial Payments
- Psychological Counseling
- PTSD Counseling
- Anger Management
- Family Counseling
- Medical care for you and your family
- Dental
- And much more!

VA Benefits and PTSD

In this chapter we will discuss VA benefits primarily as they pertain to PTSD issues. There is so much raw information regarding VA benefits out there that we could easily turn this guide into a 20 volume encyclopedia. The list of benefits available is quite long and can even include fun things like:

- Free camping and parking at State and Federal Campgrounds, Beaches, Etc
- Free fishing licenses,
- Free train and bus transportation,

I could get off on a tangent here talking about all the benefits you could be throwing away by giving up and falling through the cracks. This above should be enough to at least get you fishermen off the couch!

The rest of you need to become a lot more Trypophobic! Avoid all holes or cracks in the system.

OK. Let's get back on track!

I did mention in the first chapter that I have ADD didn't I? My publisher periodically slaps me on the back of my head and yells, **"Focus Don!"** He reminds me of those gnarly DI's (drill instructors) that I also mentioned in the first chapter

This guide is **focused** on helping you become a War Zone PTSD Survivor. It is not necessary for you to receive VA benefits to make this happen, however it sure could make life much easier for you.

I will not attempt to cover everything you need to know about the VA and VA benefits in this one guide. I will however cover the important topics as they relate to PTSD. The good news is that we back this guide up with a Website that comes with, most importantly:

PTSD Message Boards
http://www.ptsdhotline.com/forum/forum.php

Build a Study Guide to use with the PTSD Message Boards

While studying this chapter I would recommend that you have a pencil and pad of paper handy. You will have many questions pop up as you read on. By writing the questions down you can save them and ask your questions on our Message Boards.

Better yet type your questions out in Microsoft Word or whatever you use. For those of you online copy and paste your questions into the message boards. There are many thousands of Vets who have asked these same questions over the years and they will be glad to help you. That is why this statement below is just so important to you!

Vets Helping Vets!

Our Veteran brothers and sisters hold all the collective information that you will ever need to know regarding the VA, PTSD and other Veteran issues. Our message boards are designed to help you find what you need fast. Plug into the giant resource of the Veterans Knowledge Base every chance that you get. The most valuable information I have ever received came from my fellow veterans! You can do this in a number of ways:

- Our PTSD Message Boards (Link Above)
- Go to any VA and strike up conversations with the vets you see there. This is actually fun. You can spend the day in the game rooms, libraries, and even have an inexpensive lunch at their cafeteria.

- Groups like the VFW and American Legion: You can meet many other vets there. Note: Most have active cocktail areas so keep that in mind if you have substance abuse issues.
- Military Garb: This may sound silly at first but many vets wear military shirts and hats. This means that they are proud of their military service and will be glad to talk to another vet. Start with a simple statement like "Welcome Home Brother". That always opens the door to conversation if you are open to it. I wear my Vietnam Vets hat everywhere in the hopes of meeting other vets to talk to.

Research

For much more in-depth VA Benefits information search online. Go to resources such as the United States Dept. of Veterans Affairs Website. This is a free website.

http://www.va.gov/

The above is an official government website and it is extremely in-depth. That can also mean complex. It can take a lot of work to wade through it all to cull the info that you need. They must cover everything. Most of the times you don't need literally everything to get the job done.

The book you are reading is the "**War zone PTSD Survivors Guide**". It does not go in-depth with everything you need to know about the VA. It is about helping you become a **PTSD Survivor**. Again you do not need to put in for benefits to become a PTSD Survivor. There are some other great books out there that deal strictly with VA benefits.

Below is a good one that you can find on our website at:
http://ptsdhotline.com/html/books___more.ht ml

Note: There are three underscores between the words books___words

For a much more user friendly approach to VA Benefits I would spend the money and get this book below. They didn't have books like this when I was beating my head against the machine. I had to be a dummy all by myself. The **"For Dummies"** series of books are always top notch:

"Veterans Benefits for Dummies"
by Rod Powers
Retired Air Force First Sergeant

From this book
* Health care
* Ongoing care for wounded and disabled vets
* Education assistance
* Vocational rehabilitation
* Life insurance
* Home loan guarantees
* Pensions
* Survivors' benefits
* Burial benefits

Question Do you need to have an Honorable Discharge to get VA Help and Benefits?

Answer: No!

These types of unique questions and answers are also covered in this book. Many vets who suffered from PTSD got into some trouble while still in the military. These soldiers should not be swept aside.

I got my Kindle eBook copy of it for about 10 bucks and I use the heck out of it to help other vets answer their own questions. It is definitely worth the small investment.

You can order this book as Paper Back or Ebook on our website:

WWW.PTSDHotline.Com

Back to this book – Some other topics covered in this chapter:

PTSD and Substance Abuse

Getting Service Connected benefits and finding help for your PTSD and/or Substance Abuse go hand in hand. For the purposes of this guide I can't really discuss one without the other. The most important thing here is getting you real help for the problems that war has caused you. Self-Medication with drugs and alcohol is extremely common and has been talked about a number of times in this guide already.

Can PTSD In your Permanent record cause you stigma problems?

This is a tricky question. Let's not take it lightly. Below is info taken directly from the **VA.Gov** Website that I mentioned above.

What Is Stigma?

Stigma is when you feel judged by other people because of some personal quality or trait. You may feel stigma because of negative things people say about you, or because they treat you differently. An example of stigma related to PTSD is a belief that people with PTSD are dangerous or unstable, which is not true.

Some examples of stigma include:

• Negative labels or stereotypes that assume all people with PTSD are the same

• Discrimination at work, at school, or finding housing because of your symptoms

• Being denied chances to succeed because of a PTSD diagnosis

Because of concerns about stigma, you may try to hide the problem or not admit you need care. You may start to feel that you deserve to be treated badly because of your symptoms. But PTSD is not something to be ashamed of. The best thing you can do for yourself is to take control and get help.

Barriers specific to military personnel

When you are in the military, there are other things that may get in the way of seeking help. Military members may worry that talking about PTSD with doctors, other soldiers, or commanding officers will hurt their career. You may think if people in your unit learn you have PTSD they will see you as weak, or not trust you to be able to protect them. Or, you may feel that your medical records will be opened for other people to see.

Being afraid that seeking treatment will damage your career leads you to avoid getting help at a time when you need it most. Many don't get help until their return from deployment, or when their family tells them there is a problem. But you don't have to wait.

You may think that avoiding your PTSD is critical to keeping your job. But if your PTSD symptoms are getting in the way of doing your duties, it is better to deal with them before they hurt your military career. Getting help for PTSD is problem solving.

Even though this subject above is mentioned on their website it does not come right out and give you a definitive answer as to whether PTSD in your permanent record can impact your military career or future employment in Police work, Fire Dept, etc.

Text book info says that it won't but this is real life. Is it possible to have a less than ethical person involved with the direction of your career in or out of the military? You be the judge!

Does the VA Share Information?

I can tell you that at this time if you go to the VA to ask questions and even get into a PTSD Program there is no big brother tie in of computer generated info shared between the VA, DOD (Dept. of Defense), or other organizations like the Police Dept., etc.

A friend of mine from a PTSD and Substance Abuse Program at the VA just received his Sergeants stripes. He is fighting his 2nd 502 (drunken driving charge). He also attends AA meetings. None of this impacted his advancement.

Do not allow this issue to stop you from getting help for your PTSD. You would be surprised at how many people that you personally know that are in the military, police and/or fire depts., and are also in PTSD, AA Meetings and Substance Abuse Programs. I personally know many myself because they are in programs with me at the VA. The reason you don't know this about people in your club, school or workplace is because they choose to talk about it where it counts, in a PTSD Program, and not in the lunch room or on the street!

I will continue to develop information about this important topic. It is important enough to have its own message board. Look for it at our website:

WWW.PTSDHotline.Com.

Getting back into the VA System

Climb back out of the cracks and holes in the system!

This is for those of you that want to get plugged back into the system for benefits purposes. Any of you who don't want a statement of PTSD in your permanent military record let the doctors and psychologists that you talk to know your concerns and discuss it. If you want VA benefits for PTSD you will need to get PTSD counseling and join a program. Again this is in your VA record and not others.

Specific Steps

In this next section I will give you specific steps that you need to do. Which ones you do first is up to you as long as you get them all done.

These steps worked for me and for the other vets that I have explained them to.

These steps are simplifications of what will take place but I want to make it easy for you to understand. Once you get involved with the system you will have many more questions pop up. That is why I back this whole guide up with a Website and Message Boards. Take notes!

Note: The biggest thing that stops most vets from receiving their benefits is quitting. They give up way to easily. I will mention this a number of times in this chapter. Remember - **Trypophobia** – Having a healthy fear of holes, clusters and most importantly **cracks** is a good thing in this instance!

Important Steps:

1.   Assemble any VA or Military paperwork that you have.

Before you go to the VA spend some time on this first step. Don't get overwhelmed by it and let this step stop you. Just see what you can find and put it into a file.

This will help you a lot if you can do this first but if you can't do it yourself don't worry. Go to the VA anyway without it. The important thing is to go to the VA or Vet Center to get things rolling. It is important to start a **Paper Trail** of activity relating to your issues and recovery.

If you get confused once you are there don't let that stop you either. It is quite normal to become confused. It is like learning to deal with any large institution. The Veterans Administration is one of the largest institutions in the world. Everyone goes through some form of confusion at first. The ones that stick it out are the ones who end up with help and benefits.

To go along with the paperwork try to write a simple outline of what steps you have taken in dealing with the VA in the past. This does not have to be perfect. Just try to convey what you can remember. If you have any documents that support this outline it will be helpful. You will want your **DD 214**. If you don't have it ask your Local VA to help you get one or go online here:

http://www.archives.gov/veterans/militar y-service-records/.

What is a DD Form 214?

The DD-214 is the standard separation document of the United States Military. Previous to the DD 214 there were various other Separation Documents. They are all referred to now as DD 214. Do not confuse the Discharge Certificate with the DD 214, these are two separate documents. The Discharge Certificate is for hanging on your wall. It has no official status as a document to prove military service. Only the DD-214 or its replacement (Certificate of Service) is accepted by the Military, the Social

Security Administration or the Veterans Administration to prove military service. You can use the DD 214 as the document you need for verification of employment during your military years for bank loans etc.

You may find information in your DD 214 that is wrong. **Don't panic!** You can't get the DD 214 changed but you can get an addendum to correct anything in it that is wrong. I mention this because a friend of mine, upon getting plugged back into the VA System, found things wrong in his DD 214 such as his actual MOS. It had him listed as a clerk when he was actually out in the field. This may not have caused him a problem with getting benefits for PTSD but he wanted the record straight.

Things to try to find and list

Don't let this list stop you. I keep saying don't let things stop you because so many Vets get frustrated and head back into the hills. That is a really dumb move that will continue to haunt you for the rest of your life. I didn't do the paper work compilation thing and I am still at 100%. Making a list and building files will just make your life easier and cut a ton of time off the process. I screwed around and pecked at it. That is why it took me 40 years to get to 100%. You don't need to go through it that way. You can shave years down to months!

Note: Legal Statement: I am not guaranteeing anyone 100% or even 10%. It has to do with your own personal military experiences and your desire to have your true experiences evaluated correctly. If you stay out of the cracks in the system you have a real chance to get the help that you need. If you give up you have none!

Here is a list of what type of stuff to look for:

- Any Military Records you may have including the DD 214
- Any paperwork regarding your military service.
- What health problems you have had in and out of the military. Any doctors and

hospitals you have dealt with - VA or otherwise.

- What programs, if any, that you have attended. (AA, PTSD Programs at the VA, Etc)

- List any VA benefits you may have applied for in the past even if you were turned down. The VA will also have copies of that but it doesn't hurt to go in with as much ammo in your kit as possible.

Note: Here is an example of getting at least your most basic paperwork together first and not letting things stop you or slow you down

Greg's Story:

I am working with a Gulf War vet right now who was on the verge of giving up. He has been hitting the wall with trying to take back his life. After we talked he finally decided to go take another shot at the VA.

I didn't know that he had had his wallet stolen and didn't even have a driver's license to show once he got there.

He ran into one of the PBADs (**Prisoners** Behind a Desk) that I have mentioned earlier in this guide. He said

"You don't have any ID? Sorry I can't help you. NEXT!"

What a crappy thing to do to someone who has fought for his country! Of course Greg went home upset. Thanks to this clerk (rhymes with Jerk) it was a total wasted trip and another reason to give up.

The PBAD should have directed him to the proper office at the VA to get a copy of his ID (VIC) in the works while he was already there.

Here is info about your VA ID card (VIC) from VA.Com:

The only purpose of the card is for identification and check-in at VA appointments. The VIC cannot be used as a credit card or an insurance card, and it does not authorize or pay for care at non-VA facilities.

Veterans should safeguard their VIC similar to other identification cards that contain personal information.

To receive a VIC, the Veteran must have his/her picture taken for the card at the VA Medical Facility. The card will be mailed to the Veteran within 7-10 days after the Veteran's eligibility has been verified. To ensure the VIC is received at the appropriate address, it is important that the Veteran's address is verified and the correct address is entered in the VistA computer system. If the U.S. Postal Service cannot deliver the card, it will be returned to the facility where the Veteran requested the card.

If the Veteran does not receive the card in the 7-10 day timeframe, the Veteran should contact the local VA Medical Facility where the card was requested or call VA at 1-877-222-VETS (8387)

Thank God Greg is still going at it! He is getting his VIC and moving on with fighting for his benefits. Sometimes it does seem to be a fight but we're warriors so no giving up allowed! They taught us to fight so go ahead and use it in a constructive way!

2. To get rolling you can go to the local VA Hospital, VA Clinics, or to a Vet Center. I recommend going right to the horse's mouth – The VA. Now I know some of you would consider the VA as another part of the horse's anatomy!☺ Let's play nice! After reading this guide and arming yourself with paper work and good info you will find the VA a much better & easier place to deal with than you remember.

The important thing is to get started. This will start building a paper trail. **Important:** Keep track of what you do and who you talk to. As you get more involved with the system it will help keep you from doing some steps twice.

Why a paper trail? This will help you with your benefits. The VA won't take you seriously if you don't attempt to start getting help. This is particularly true with older vets that haven't been to the VA in many years. The old "Out of

Sight, Out of Mind" thing comes into play. They look at it as it must not have bothered you enough to seek help.

Service Connected

You will hear the term Service Connected or Service Connected Disability a lot. Here is a basic definition taken from the Department of Veterans Affairs. They always like to speak in legalese so pick it apart.

General Info - Service connection connotes many factors but basically it means that the facts, shown by evidence, establish that a particular injury or disease resulting in disability was incurred coincident with service in the Armed Forces, or if preexisting such service, was aggravated therein.

This may be accomplished by affirmatively showing inception or aggravation during service or through the application of statutory presumptions. Each disabling condition shown by a veteran's service records, or for which he seeks a service connection must be considered on the basis of the places, types and circumstances of his service as shown by service records.

The official history of each organization in which he served, his medical records and all pertinent medical and lay evidence. Determinations as to service connection will be based on review of the entire evidence of record, with due consideration to the policy of the Department of Veterans Affairs to administer the law under a broad and liberal interpretation consistent with the facts in each individual case.

Basically it means that the more info you have about your medical issues and how they relate to your military service the better. The Department of Veterans Affairs and the VA should have all your records available but again be Proactive. Help them along as best you can.

It is very smart to make an extra copy of all your records to keep in a safe place.

Appoint an Advocate/Representative

This is a decision you should put some thought and extra time into. I did not go this route but as I have said it took me many more years than I want to see it take you. You will hear over and over again from me the term **"Become Proactive"** in your recovery. This is one of those times. Don't just go with the first person you talk to. I recommend talking with several different reps and to go with the one that seems the sharpest. Ask other local vets who they think is a good rep at your local VA and go talk to them. Reps gain a reputation for their positive good work.

I know guys that had their benefits delayed or denied and much time lost due to a Rep not filling out the paperwork correctly or filing it with wrong info attached.

I also know of many vets that made mistakes on their paperwork trying to do it themselves. In other words this is an important time for you to pay attention. When a rep does your paperwork make sure that the information he or she has to work with is accurate. Double check the forms with them.

There are many great people working as reps, but don't strictly rely on others. The advocates have helped many thousands of vets but keep in mind that I have met veterans who did not get a good rep at first. You need a rep that is reasonably organized. Reps have to deal with many vets and once you are out of sight they will be on to the next vet.

In other words if you get a rep don't wait too long to see that things are progressing. You should personally check their paperwork. Tell them you need a copy of anything they plan to file. Don't be afraid to ask for copies that you can review. You want to be nice and pleasant but let them know that you are active in what is going on with your claim. It doesn't hurt to become "The Squeaky Wheel". Just don't become the Screaming one.

While there are attorneys who will represent you for a fee, it is rarely necessary to pay to have your claim processed efficiently and successfully. First try National Service

Organizations such as these. They all have reps for you to work with:

- Disabled American Veterans
- Veterans of Foreign Wars
- American Legion
- Vietnam Veterans of America
- Paralyzed Veterans of America
- Purple Heart Foundation

Most of these organizations have an office at many of the VA Hospitals. Most towns have an American Legion, VFW, etc. Contact them and ask questions.

Also State Departments of Veterans Affairs or Veterans Commissions and County Veteran Service Officers can give excellent assistance and it's free. Call your local regional office to see what organizations and services are available at that office. Always make notes.

Most of them will help you start your claim but there are also ways to electronically file if you are into using the Internet. This link below is long so if you have this guide online click on it or copy and paste it into your address bar of your browser. If not type it carefully into your browser with no spaces and watch for the underscores:

https://www.ebenefits.va.gov/ebenefits-portal/ebenefits.portal?_nfpb=true&_portlet.asy nc=false&_pageLabel=ebenefits _myeb_vonapp1

Note: You can also find this link & other important ones in the section on VA Benefits on our website WWW.PTSDHotline.Com.

Go to the section on Benefits:
http://ptsdhotline.com/html/va___benefits.html
Note: In the link above the gap between va___benefits is three underscores

3.   Take your records and go to your local VA or Vet Center now!

If you already have representatives ask them about these steps below. I would use these steps anyway to go along with what the Rep does. Mainly the Rep will help you fill out and file the forms. You will want to stay proactive in all the rest. It doesn't hurt to have several avenues of approach as long as it doesn't get you confused with too much info. By keeping a list of the steps you have taken it will keep you on track.

At the VA or Vet Center ask to talk to someone about VA benefits and getting plugged into a program involving PTSD. They will give you info on what to do. They may direct you to another office within the VA. Take a pad of paper and write down what they say. Some VA Hospitals are huge and sprawling. It is easy to get lost if you don't take notes on where you want to go next. Ask for a copy of a map of this VA. Most will have one and they can show you where to go next.

Physical:

If it is your first time or has been a long time since you have seen a doctor at the VA tell them you need a basic physical. Getting plugged back into the system will require a physical. This is definitely for your benefit. Take advantage of any free tests that you can get. Even the ones where they start by pulling on a rubber glove!☺

This will add to the paper trail, which is what you want to do. It is always of benefit to you to know if you have any medical problems that should be looked into.

The sooner you can get into a weekly meeting involving PTSD and/or Substance Abuse, the better. If you get into other programs like Anger Management make sure they have a system in place that checks you into the meetings. Make sure you remember to always check in! Many vets forget to do this and it will negatively impact their paper trail when nothing gets filed.

Remember this guide is for PTSD. I am giving you a progression that works for that. If you had a broken arm or heart problems I would give you a totally different approach.

Also remember that if you want benefits you have to show that you are willing to work at your recovery. Building a paper trail is extremely important. It may take you 6 months or more to get your benefits but once you have put in the claim you will be back paid to the date you started this claim.

Do people get turned down? Yes! My advice to you is to never take no for an answer. Re-apply the same day or the next. The sooner the better! That will show them that you are serious about having a problem and show that you intend to be Proactive with the situation.

Sometimes I wonder if they automatically turn people down the first time to weed out the people that are not serious enough. Is that another pesky crack to watch out for? Jump it!

This is not farfetched. It happens at many agencies. I was turned down the first time I went in for my Social Security Disability. I went to see a lawyer. I was told to put in for them again as most lawyers won't even take your case until after you have been turned down at least twice. In the case of Social Security you don't always get back paid. Doesn't take much of an imagination to become somewhat skeptical toward the games that are being played!

Being the Squeaky Wheel

I knew a Vet that worked on his case with **intention**. He kept a file of everything that happened at the VA including doctors' appointments, meetings he attended and even a record of phone conversations he had with reps.

As he continued to go to the VA the file became thicker and thicker. Every time he went into the VA he handed them a full multi page copy of the ever expanding file including the latest pages. It forced them to continue to copy every single page each time he did this. The VA doesn't believe in saving trees! They copy everything. That was a ton of work for a PBAD. Was that a squeaky wheel? Yes. Did they remember him? You bet! Did he get benefits? Yes! They got tired of copying his file☺☺☺. That one deserves 3 smiley faces!

This was many years ago and I don't know if that would work today but the point is to get involved with your case and stay Proactive in your recovery.

Monthly Income

Getting financial help is why many vets want to get plugged back into the system but the good news is that to do that they actually get help for things they didn't even realize they needed. Once they start going to meetings a very important thing happens. They come to realize that all the things that they have been going through are not just happening to them alone. Realizing **"You are not Alone"** is such a relief and becomes extremely important to your recovery!!! They didn't even know they had PTSD. They didn't know what PTSD meant!

I hear that all the time from other Vets. It is such a breath of fresh air for them to realize that what they are experiencing is not solely happening to them. The meetings become their **Safe Harbor** and they build great friendships among the vets that they meet. It becomes easy to share your issues with vets who have shared their own issues with you.

Another big reason Vets want to get plugged in is because they have legal trouble such as a Drunk Driving ticket. Does it help them with their case? In many cases yes it does. The good news again is that they start getting help and find out for the first time that they have problems caused by PTSD. It doesn't matter what gets you to the VA or Vet Center. What matters is that you have made a giant step forward in your recovery.

4. Travel Pay, Vic ID Card and more

I put this topic next for those of you that live a distance from your VA. You will want to get this handled early in the process due to the insane gas prices we have today. As of this writing $4.10 a gallon reg. unleaded. This is important to you especially once you get into weekly meetings.

Not all of you will be eligible for Travel Pay that is why you will want to fill out a **Means Test**. Simply ask for the form next time you are at the VA. It is a simple form to determine whether you make too much money to have any co-pay costs waived for visits and meds. It also can qualify you for travel pay if you are under 30% Service Connected.

You may not be eligible for things like Travel Pay until you reach 30% Service Connected. You can also become eligible if you can prove that driving to the VA would cause a financial hardship on you.

At most VA's your ID Card (VIC), Means Test and more can be handled in one office and in one visit. It is usually all in the same building. Bring paper and pen. Take notes on where to go next! This will save you from tons of confusion and extra time. I keep saying this because it will really save you time and energy. It is easy to become confused. We're Vets☺

As mentioned above you will want to get a **VA Photo ID Card (VIC)**. Ask about it. Generally you can get your VA Photo ID in the same place you get Travel Pay Info as well.

Once you establish your eligibility for Travel Pay you will want to go back to the Travel Pay office. I wouldn't make a special trip to do that as you won't get travel pay for that trip. Wait until your next scheduled meeting. Better yet bring these things below with you the first time you go to the VA. Why not **"Get R Done!"**

- To start getting Travel Pay bring proof of car insurance and proof of address, such as a utility bill in your name. Once eligible you will receive round trip travel based upon the mileage amount that is current. At this writing it is approximately 41.5 cents per mile. You will have to prove your home address once every 6 months.
- Bring your banking information. Bank account # and routing #. Most of the VA's now do direct deposit for things like Travel Pay

You may not get travel pay if you take a bus or other public transportation. Once you get Service Connected Benefits you may be eligible for free public transportation. I am 100% so in California I get free Amtrak Train and pickup at my door from certain shuttle services. There are so many other ancillary benefits available to you that I won't go into them all in this guide. I am putting all that type of info into our website: WWW.PTSDHotline.Com. You may be eligible for things like:

- Free Public Transportation: Busses, Trains & more....
- Free Hunting and Fishing Licenses
- Free Campsites
- Care Giver Compensation
- And much more

If you don't have a scheduled appointment but need to see a doctor for an emergency you can receive travel pay for ½ or in other words the return trip. I am not certain why this is so but possibly to stop some from making the trip everyday just to receive the travel pay.

There will always be people that take advantage of the system. That makes it harder for the rest of us!

Here is a link to much more info: http://www.columbiamo.va.gov/Travel_Reimbu rsement.asp. If you have this PTSD Guide online you can click on it or copy and paste it into your browser.

5. Put in for Service Connected Benefits ASAP

We have gone over some of this already in Step 3 but let's go over it again in more detail. Now that you have done the steps in the Bulleted List below you may want to write or type a quick outline of them with notes on who you have dealt with.

You may be asked a few times what you have done so far, what doctors you have already seen as you continue to see new doctors or PBADs. It will impress them and let them know that you are serious and intend to follow up. Having this outline will save you a bunch of time not having to remember it all off the top of your head. Have several copies and hand them one. Impressive!

OK you have done these things:

- **Assembled all the paperwork that you can**
- ***Appointed an Advocate/Representative**
- **Filled out a Means Test and received a (VIC) ID Card**
- **Applied for Travel Pay** (if applicable)
- **Have seen a doctor: Note** - Ask the doctor to give you a written (or computer generated) referral to a PTSD program. This will help you save a lot of time. Make sure once you have the referral to contact the person that will set you up with meetings. Most VA's have a gate keeper type of person that will schedule you into a group.
- **Had a physical: Note** – Ask the first doctor you talk to in the above step about the physical,
- **Joined a program such as weekly PTSD meetings**

  Note: This sounds like a lot but a number of these things can be done in one visit to the VA.

Ready Go! Now that you have done the things above it is now the best time to put in a **Claim** for your PTSD benefits. If you have service connected benefits already in place but not for PTSD open a new claim ASAP. If you have service connected benefits in place for PTSD already but feel that you deserve a higher percentage re-file a claim! I did this a number of times and with my growing paper trail I continued to get upgrades. I started at 15% and am now 100%.

Again appointing a representative to file your claim can be extremely helpful. There are some great ones you can find in the list of associations below but don't appoint one and then set back.

Follow up and be sure that they submitted all your papers correctly. You will receive acknowledgement papers within weeks. If you don't than dig back in and ask your rep - **"What's Up!"**

Here again are some organizations that can help you file a claim:

- **Disabled American Veterans**
- **Veterans of Foreign Wars**
- **American Legion**
- **Vietnam Veterans of America**
- **Paralyzed Veterans of America**
- **State Departments of Veterans Affairs or Veterans Commissions and County Veteran Service Officers**

You can also go into your local VA and ask for help in filing a claim for Service Connected Benefits.

In other words it is easy to find help in filing once you decide to do it. You can even do it online.

Here is a great place to file an informal claim with the VA and lock in the date. This is important because if you win your claim you will get back paid to that date:

http://benefits.va.gov/transformation/fastclaims/?gclid=CP6Kp9SkvacCFSFpgwod9kENNA

Don't muddy the water

Know what you are putting your claim in for. In the case of people reading this guide you are more than likely putting in a claim for PTSD.

Here are tips from Tom Pamperin of the VA – His blog dated 1/04/2011:

Consider what you want to claim. Many Service members and veterans have been told they should go through their service medical records and claim everything they have ever had or been treated for. While you can do that, it is likely to significantly increase your frustration level, result in unnecessary examinations, and slow the process without getting added benefits. You should not claim acute disabilities or illnesses you had in service unless they left a residual.

For example, if you got the flu in service and got over it, the claim will be denied. On the other hand if you broke your leg and recovered from it you should claim that because the fracture, if found on x-ray, can be service connected. While it might only warrant a zero percent evaluation now, if you develop arthritis at the site later, you are covered.

Don't claim things like personality disorders, baldness, the fact that you wear glasses or similar kinds of things because they are considered "constitutional or developmental abnormalities" that you would have gotten whether or not you were in service. The law doesn't permit payment for these.

Don't claim lab results like hematuria (blood in the urine) or high cholesterol. We don't pay for those either. On the other hand, you should claim pseudofolliculitis barbae (a skin condition that affects some black people).

Author's Note This below is a different Tom than the VA's Tom Pamperin above.

Tom W's Story

An example of muddying the water is a Vietnam Marine Vet I know who I have mentioned earlier in this guide. He has a number of problems that are service connected.

He is down to using ½ a lung due to Agent Orange. He is also dealing with a powerful dose of PTSD. He has tried many times to get benefits for Agent Orange.

Even though he has write-ups from outside doctors stating that he has Agent Orange in his system the VA won't recognize Agent Orange unless it is accompanied by Diabetes. He was turned down and received zero for his efforts. This is another of those truly crappy Catch 22 things that seem to crop up everywhere in the Military and the Government.

He had all the criteria for exhibiting a strong case for PTSD. He was beating his head against the powers that be regarding his Agent Orange. This was causing him anger and frustration. He gave up and didn't go back to the VA for a number of years. Yep the cracks got him.

After talking to me he is now concentrating on getting Service Connected Benefits for his PTSD instead. It is like the old saying, "Tomato or Tomahto". As long as he gets 80% to 100% for one or the other it still works to his benefit. Better yet instead of fighting the Agent Orange thing which was causing him anger and anguish he is now getting real help for his PTSD. If he had continued to mix Agent Orange Issues with his PTSD that would have muddied things up for years to come.

Author's Note: 8/1/2012 Tom just contacted me at the Sepulveda, California VA while we were there at a PTSD Meeting. He has just received 40% for his PTSD and a large check for back pay on it. He is also getting back paid for his Travel and he is being reimbursed for the $15.00 per meeting co-pay that he had been making for his weekly PTSD Meetings.

What is really exciting is that I had told him to put in for a Purple Heart that he had not received due to bazaar circumstances. He is now set up to receive his medal and it looks really good. I think he is more excited about the medal than the money.

He is already putting in for an upgrade to the 40%. He did this within days! Good for him! With all the problems he has experienced from Agent Orange and PTSD he deserves 100%!

Everywhere he goes he has to carry an oxygen tank. I find this type of situation more than enough to get me up in the morning to buck a system that sometimes seems unfair.

This type of vindication for the volunteer work that my wife and I do is all the payment we will ever need. It proves that what I am telling you to do works! So get off the couch and head to your local VA today!

Now that hurts patting myself on the back so hard☺

I myself have some other medical issues due to being wounded 5 times and incurring Hepatitis due to the Army accidentally put me in a Hepatitis ward when I had many open wounds. I could put in other claims but I am at 100% already. So what would be the point?

It is possible to get over 100% and receive more money but I am happy with what I have.

Getting involved with the PTSD Programs was the best thing I ever could have done for myself and for my family and friends as well. The way I can tell this is because I still have family and friends in my life!

Here is more info below from Tom Pamperin's Blog relating to what paperwork you will receive from the VA. If you don't receive this in a reasonable time period, several months or less, contact your rep or the person who helped you submit your claim.

Tom's Pamperin's Blog (Again Different Tom than the Agent Orange Tom just above)

The first thing you will get from the VA once you file your claim is a lengthy letter commonly referred to as a "VCAA letter." This is a letter required by the law that tells you what we will do, what you will be expected to do, and in very general terms tell you how we will decide. The letter may also include specific requests from your local regional office for information. Read it carefully for specific requests for information from us. Finally, the letter offers the option of completing an attachment telling us you have no more information. If that is the case, complete the form and return it immediately. If you don't and you have no more information, we will wait for 30 days before proceeding for no good reason. Even if, during the course of working the claim you do get additional information you can always submit it when you get it.

For more of Tom's blog go to

http://www.blogs.va.gov/VAntage/1089/ some-tips-for-filing-a-va-disability-claim/.

If you are reading this online click on it or copy and paste it into your browser. If you are reading this in hard copy then copy it carefully into your browser.

Author's Note: This blog is still online as of May 2012. It is so good that I am going to add it to our website with a link to the growing list of responses.

This Blog has excellent responses from vets and others. They are full of info that can help you. At the end of this chapter I have included a few of the over 600 responses. I left them as is with spelling mistakes and all. They are full of great nuggets of information.

Care Giver Benefits:

In cases where a vet is 100% Service Connected and can't get around on his own, feed or clothe himself he/or she may receive financial help for a Care Giver that can even be their spouse or a family member. I know Vets whose wives or family members receive $600 per month as their caregiver. Find out more: http://www.caregiver.va.gov/

There is a lot more info available regarding VA Benefits. The info in this guide relates to benefits regarding PTSD and hit the high spots.

Go to our Message Boards to ask your questions:
http://www.ptsdhotline.com/forum/forum.php

Claim Denied

As mentioned above in this chapter claims do get denied.

Do not take "No" for an answer!

Here is another book that I highly recommend:

Maj. John D. Roche, USAF (Ret.)

Maj. John D. Roche, USAF (Ret.), served as a bomber pilot, had combat duty in the Korean and Vietnam Wars, and held a variety of administrative assignments. Subsequently, he worked for sixteen years as a claims adjudicator specialist for the Veterans Administration and as a veterans' service officer for Pinellas County, Florida, where he was a tireless advocate for veterans and their families. Roche enjoyed one of the highest rates of wins on appeal in the state. This book is based on his experience as a successful practitioner, many years of independent research, and personal consultations with some 80,000 veterans, widows, and dependents.

You can order this book as Paper Back or Ebook on our website:

WWW.PTSDHotline.Com

Here are a few of the comments on Tom Pamperins blog from above:

684 Comments "Some Tips for Filing a VA Disability Claim"

* *Wayne Bufford* says:
January 4, 2011 at 9:51 p.m.

Also check you DD214, the person who filled mine out did not take the time to turn the page of my records to say I served overseas in Vietnam! Had to fight to get that cleared up. finally got my medals after filing and asking for them, they were approved but never issued to me during my service. I got them 2 years after requesting them. If you are hurt or have PTSD, if they say no the first time, Keep your records and doctor's records and keep filing appeals.

Check with your state to see if they have a state funded commission who has vets to help vets free of charge to get the appeals filed correctly and on time. If it goes to a hearing they will go with you and they will fight for you. We did not have any luck with the group at the VA Hospital who was supposed to help me get my compensation for
serving or for my disability now.
God Bless Brother and Sister, Welcome Home! Keep fighting!

- *Berta Simmons* says:
January 5, 2011 at 9:52 am

Excellent article! Thank you very much Mr. Pamperin!
Keeping the claim simple (as you indicated)is a big help too. Focus on the primary potential SC disabilities and then add what are possible secondary's to each primary. But be reasonable. Claims that involve 15 or 20 issues make my eyes glaze over, as a veteran's advocate, so I imagine a rater would feel the same way too.
I totally agree with Jim too, in everything he said   here.
I always tell vets that the best service rep they will ever have is the person they see in their

bathroom mirror every morning. They must be proactive with their claim whether they have a vet rep or not.

Vet reps handle hundreds of claims (and maybe even thousands that are still in appellate processes) but veterans or survivors usually have only one main claim that could have some additional issues.

This article is a MUST read for all of us! I am printing this out as well as passing it on.

Thank you again!

- *Dylan Finsand* says:
  March 6, 2011 at 4:36 am

  Being your own best rep isn't always true. I have a TBI with dementia. Some have serious cognitive problems and are not their best rep. I've had VSO and good people at VA tell Dylan don't ever do anything on your own with your claims again! Just something to keep in mind. Thanks for reading

- *Thomas J Dittmar* says:
  January 7, 2011 at 10:35 p.m.

  Sir, I filed a Gulf War illness claim with the Seattle RO in the 90's but the Gulf War illness claim was deferred in the 90's with no further contact by VA. I re-filed the claim March of

2010. Approximately 2 months ago I received a notice that I would be contacted by VA medical for an exam but never heard another word. Can someone explain to me what is happening with my re-file? I don't want this claim to be lost like the one in the 90's

- *SCOTT PRATER* says:
January 8, 2011 at 11:28 p.m.

It would be best to contact the local regional office and make sure they actually received the claim and supporting documents. Call 1-800-827-1000 and it will send your call from the switch to you local office. I select 1 when finally given the option and 0 for general assistance. It can take different lengths of time but they can make a decision on your claim, or usually they sent a request to a company called QTC who will send you to an unbiased doctor to see you and possible run tests to support your claim. If it has been sent to QTC you will be told so and can get the headquarters number and ask for info from them if they have scheduled you and appt. or what the status is. The VA reps also may need to ask you questions and input them in the system or transfer your call to someone able to record needed info related to your claim so it can move forward. Hope this helps.

Scott

- *Dylan Finsand* says:

March 10, 2011 at 11:44 p.m.

Or VA is looking at it and are gonna tell you that its not service connected because they have a habit of not having all your records. But most likely it waiting in line with everyone else's cause it does take time.

☐ *Bekki* says:

September 22, 2011 at 6:38 p.m.

My husband has filed a claim twice and once the person that in the claim review office told him that since he is a Vietnam Vet he is on the back burner and the service men and women that are coming home now have priority..... Let's think about this a minute if is wasn't for those who have served in Vietnam we wouldn't have the service men and women fighting now.... That is how back words our Government really is. We are still waiting, and the last time we put in a claim was years ago.

☐ *Miguel Cucue* says:

December 6, 2011 at 6:17 p.m.

Bekki,

I am one of those soldiers who just returned from our current war. I honestly agree with you and that is WRONG! Veterans from older wars should have priority. The government's system is all messed up! My best goes out to you, your husband and your family. Keep fighting because I am still battling to get my claim going.

☐ *Carmen Tellez* says:
March 3, 2012 at 4:18 am

Mr. Michael Cucue:

You're absolutely correct every veteran needs to be recognized/compensated for their service to our country. My late husband served in Korea (front lines) for 3 years. Frank came home 12/54, we met 12/71 and married 6/71. After our son was born, he was born with Cerebral Palsy and Autism, not easy but through love and lots of patience he's very functional but still needs supervision. Frank was diagnosed with PTSD 3/93 but it took VA till 11/2004 to admit it was due to war. He passed away on 4/16/2010 because of PTSD. We were sure that our son and I would be compensated nicely instead we have been denied all benefits except commissary. What's wrong with this government?

My apologies for wordy letter, I'm angry and hurt, we were married 38 years, and please advice if possible.
My heartfelt thanks,
Carmen Tellez
An angry & hurt veterans widow.

☐ *Romy A.* says:

January 12, 2012 at 2:23 p.m.

It is very frustrating for a Viet Nam veteran like me as well because we did not get separation briefing at all to explain our benefits. Now, it seems like all help are concentrated to other war era veterans. Presumed illnesses are hardly applied to the Viet Nam vets unless one served close or in mainland for the Agent Orange issue. I think VA should be more open minded and really look at the illnesses claimed if the job can be related to that. Outside doctors (PPOs) only keep their patients' record for the most 5 years. So, a vet like me is out luck for securing those records as proof for the claim.

☐ *Halrow* says:

March 1, 2012 at 3:11 p.m.

Hello, I'm also a Vietnam combat veteran......You say your husband is a Viet Vet and his claim is taking a long time. The truth is, that his

VA medical Record and DD214 needs to be intact and in the hands

of the VA or the organization representing your Veteran husband.

Having said that, I can tell you that claims that have real and lawful

entitlements to a veteran by way of his service connected health

issues should be readily provided to the entitled veteran as

earned compensation. The matter of taking a long time, may be

a hardship issue to some older and more seriously ill vets. However

it should be noted by you Bekki, that a legal veterans compensation

award is paid retroactive to the date the VA acknowledges the

initial receipt of your husband's claim. In other words for every

month that passes on a pending claim the veteran gets paid when

the claim is finally awarded. Having said that, it should be noted that

any retroactive award payment, of course

depends on the amount,
determined by the service connected disability anywhere from
10% to 100% . I wish you and your husband all the best wishes
and hope this takes some pressure off you and any entitled vets
who suffer from poor sleep and probable PTSD and stress
related health issues. I'm getting stressed myself right now, and
must keep watching my blood pressure. After 6 long life threatening
surgeries. And a low life of 40 I need to take life a bit more casually
these days. I like helping others though, so i hope this message
helps.

- *John* says:

September 14, 2011 at 6:18 am

The best thing you could ever possibly do is get your DD214, your doctors/hospitals' names, addresses, phone numbers and contact your closest Disabled American Veteran organization for a service officer and have them represent you. Doing it alone, no matter how much documentation you have, can be totally fruitless.

- *Laura* says:
<u>September 19, 2011 at 1:11 am</u>

My uncle was in Vietnam. He was blown up, exposed to Agent Orange and still has metal in his body. He never filed and cannot take off work because the money he does bring in doesn't cover his bills as it is. What can I do to help him?

◻ *Melissa* says:
<u>October 13, 2011 at 10:31 am</u>

He can contact a service organization by phone and they can send him out the paperwork and help him get started. If I assist a veteran in this situation, I try to give them as much info as I can over the phone, mail them the forms, have them fill them out and send back to me for review. If there are areas that need to be addressed, my assistant or I call the veteran and get those areas clarified. The vet will eventually have to have to take off to attend any exams the VA schedules, but those would be the only time he would have to miss work. My service organization is Military Order of the Purple

Heart. We have National Service Officers in most states. You can check out our website at http://www.PurpleHeart.org and find the nearest representative to you, if you are interested in our assistance.

- *joseph roe* says:
  September 20, 2011 at 5:21 am
  I was told several years ago that i suffered from PTSD. Soon after I was seeing another doctor and they would not diagnose. They say I have depression. I've been suffering for 15 years and 1 out of many doctors said I had a service related illness. After that they refused to diagnose me.

☐ *Aledia Jones White* says:
March 29, 2012 at 5:58 p.m.
Get to your local VA clinic. Explain it all to your primary care physician. They will then set up an appointment with the VA mental health clinic. They are very good and well experienced at recognizing PTSD. I wish you well.

I would have loved to add all 600+ responses but there isn't enough room. The responses bring up many interesting questions and in

many cases great answers that I recommend following this blog!
http://www.blogs.va.gov/VAntage/1089/some-tips-for-filing-a-va-disability-claim/

I will continue to keep tabs on this blog on our website:
WWW.PTSDHotline.Com

Next Chapter: Physical Health

Here you will find great information on how important your body is to your recovery.

Part 2

Chapter 6
The Mental Muscle
Self-Hypnosis, Meditation, & More

Why is there a Part Two?

Part 2 is an extension of what you need to become a **War Zone PTSD Survivor.**

Everything before this chapter will give you the information you need to kick PTSD to the curb. It will also give you important steps toward receiving your much needed VA Benefits.

These next few chapters will give you additional tools that can keep you on track for the rest of your life.

Recap

You are now hopefully enrolled into PTSD Programs. You have put in for Service Connected Benefits. Things are getting better. You are taking your life back.

Author's Note I am at this stage with all of you. I have control over my PTSD issues. I now have a good relationship with the VA. I have great VA benefits across the board.

I now work hard to control my other issues as well. I still have my battles with food and drink. I love to cook and eat great food. I love mayonnaise, peanut butter, rich sauces and pizza calls out to me every time I drive by a good Italian restaurant. Well actually even when I drive by a hole in the wall pizza joint I hear, "Don, come in and get me big boy!" I still would like to have a big glass of beer or wine with that greasy slice of heaven. I have to let out another notch on my belt just driving by the place!

I have another 30 or so pounds to lose. The next couple of chapters are for my benefit. The research and work helps me toward my goal of living a healthier life. I hope you get some useful information out of these next chapters as well.

Life in the Fast Lane

First let's talk about how important a calm mind is to our Health and Physical Wellbeing.

Have you ever noticed that you are someplace you should be enjoying yet you feel antsy and want to rush on to the next peak of the roller-coaster thrill ride that your life has become?

Does this sound like your average day? You rush around for 10 hours like the Mad Hatter gobbling sacks of grease at the fast food shack, smoking cigarettes and drowning your stomach in gallons of double espresso laced coffee drinks. All of a sudden it's 8p.m. and it's time to slow the runaway train down with some good stiff shots of Jack Daniels.

You spend the night with 4 or 5 hours of tossing and turning just to pull yourself out of bed in the morning and start it all over again. Does this sound like **DEATH Race 2000** or what?

Thinking about living like this for just one more day sounds awful to me now. I used to live that way 24/7. That is if you can call this living. So why do most people do it every day for years like I did? I still can't believe looking back that I considered this a normal life. There is that word **Normal** again that we talked about in earlier chapters.

People then wonder why they don't feel so good the next day. A little "Hair of the Dog" and another day on the roller- coaster begins. We are all shocked when a doctor tells us we have heart disease or cancer.

Let's talk about some healthy ways to slow it all down

Breathing as a tool

Learning to breathe and to enjoy the moment will add years to your life. Besides making you feel good proper breathing helps your body in some real and physical ways as well. Deep relaxing breathing helps to move the lymph system, which powers up your body's cleansing mechanism. Deep breathing pushes the toxins through the Lymphatic System at a much faster rate. Now there is a fast lane that is good for you.

Deep breathing and giving yourself a little space to feel good at this moment and at this time is more important than you may think. Practice taking a look around and finding something in this moment to be happy about. I like having something around like photos of my grandkids. Even if I am on a smoggy freeway stuck in traffic this still puts a smile on my face.

Below are a couple of great ways to give you the space that you need

Self-Hypnosis

Just typing that makes me feel better.

Learning to calm yourself through self-hypnosis will help you slow down and dump the bad habits that are killing you all at the same time.

Self-Hypnosis and Meditation will help you lose weight, have a good night's sleep and enjoy where you happen to be right now no matter where you are in your life.

If you love your brain and body then set them free!

You can free up all kinds of bad habits by just learning to calm down and think about your life with intention.

A great way to use Intention to think your way to good health is with Self-Hypnosis. Once you learn to place yourself into a self-induced hypnotic state your brain can really orchestrate some major positive changes.

The Subconscious Mind

The subconscious mind doesn't argue. Give it good or bad information and it files it away equally. With a little practice you can fool your subconscious mind into dumping the bad info and replacing it with all good positive life affirming tasks such as:

- Quitting Smoking, Drugs and Alcohol
- Losing excess weight
- A desire to exercise
- Learning to study

- Dumping Road Rage or other bad habits that PTSD causes

Self-Hypnosis is such an enjoyable time for me that I look forward to it. I am not an expert but I know how well this works for me. It doesn't have to be a big deal with a ton of research. I have a simple scenario that fits my comfort zone.

For those of you that would like more in-depth information I highly recommend "Self Hypnosis for Dummies." The "For Dummies" series of books are always well researched, reliable and top notch.

I paid around $10 for this on my Kindle Reader. It is really easy to read and is chock full of great Grounding Type techniques that are so important to keeping PTSD in check. It got me back on track to losing that last 30 or 40 pounds I mentioned earlier.

On our website I will give you some good books on several subjects like this. As I have said before this guide is to help you become a Warzone PTSD Survivor. These other subjects can be a study unto themselves.

To take advantage of them you don't need to become an expert. Learn some simple basics and relax into them. This is not the time to get up tight with massive study and research. That is why the "For Dummies" is just right.

Below is another **"Stress Free Study"**. The whole purpose of these topics is to calm your mind. Can you say OHMMMMM...........?

"Meditation for Dummies"

You can order this book as Paper Back or EBook on our website:

WWW.PTSDHotline.Com

Meditation

I am relatively new to meditation. The subject has come up several times in some of the PTSD Programs that I deal with at the VA. Perhaps we should take a look at it together. A psychiatrist who I have respect for at the Sepulveda, California VA has had some positive things to say about meditation as it pertains to

PTSD. Let's see what we can find out. Also it will be a good subject for our message boards.

Meditation is a huge topic. The more I look into it the larger the subject becomes. Some of it can get a little interesting with beads and chanting and a lot of esoteric things like that. I know I am dealing with a bunch of crusty old (and young) vets here so I will limit my research to Meditation and how it can help with PTSD Issues.

I found this info below at a website that tied in Meditation, PTSD and the Military. I have heard about Transcendental Meditation for years so let's take a look at it.

Author's Note: I have no affiliation with this website or their teachings.

From their website:
PTSD and Transcendental Meditation

Surviving a traumatic event such as combat, an earthquake or a violent personal assault can be psychologically devastating. On one hand, you're alive, but the experience haunts you through flashbacks or nightmares.

You're constantly on edge and easily startled. You may feel intense guilt — or the opposite, numbness. The diagnosis: Post-traumatic Stress Disorder (PTSD).

The Transcendental Meditation (TM) technique has been scientifically demonstrated to relieve the symptoms of PTSD. The *Journal of Counseling and Development* published a study on Vietnam War veterans suffering from PTSD showing that after three months of practicing the Transcendental Meditation technique, symptoms such as anxiety, depression, family problems and alcohol usage decreased significantly. Several subjects returned to work after years of being unable to hold a job.

"I feel after I meditate that I no longer have the same intensity of tension, rage and guilt inside—it's as if a huge burden has been lifted," stated a study participant.

Why is the TM technique so effective? It eliminates the source of PTSD – stress in the mind and body.

The TM technique provides profound relaxation allowing the body to naturally dissolve deeply rooted stresses. The mind is settled, yet quietly aware during meditation.

This unique state of restful alertness refreshes and rejuvenates the mind and body. Many meditators report feeling calmer and less anxious after just a few meditations.

More than 600 research studies indicate the benefits of the TM technique such as:

- Twice as effective in reducing anxiety as other relaxation techniques such as the Relaxation Response, Progressive Muscle Relaxation, EMG Biofeedback
- Reduced substance abuse
- Increased calmness
- Decreased insomnia
- Reduction in high blood pressure
- For more info do a search for: Transcendental Meditation

This from Wikipedia

Transcendental Meditation (TM) refers to a specific form of mantra meditation called the Transcendental Meditation technique and an organization called the Transcendental Meditation movement. The TM technique and TM movement were introduced in India in the mid-1950s by Maharishi Mahesh Yogi (1914–2008).

The Maharishi personally taught thousands of people during a series of world tours to promote his teachings and developed a program to train TM teachers. Scientific research and celebrity endorsements helped to popularize Transcendental Meditation in the 1960s and 1970s and organizations were created to address different segments of the population including business people and students.

By the late 2000s, TM had been taught to millions of people and its movement had grown to include educational programs, health products and related services offered in multiple countries.

In the 1950s, the Transcendental Meditation movement was presented as a religious organization. In 1977, the Transcendental Meditation technique was held to be a religion in a New Jersey court case. By the 1970s, the organization had shifted to a more scientific presentation while maintaining many religious elements in an attempt to appeal to the more secular West.

Practitioners of Transcendental Meditation assert that their movement is not religious and describe it as a spiritual and scientific organization. The TM movement has programs and holdings in multiple countries while as many as 6 million people have been trained in the TM technique, including The Beatles, Howard Stern, Clint Eastwood, Mike Love, Russell Brand, Oprah Winfrey, David Lynch and other well-known public figures.

TM is one of the most widely practiced, and among the most widely researched meditation techniques. Research reviews of benefits for the TM technique show results ranging from inconclusive to clinically significant. Skeptics have called TM or its associated theories and technologies a pseudoscience.

Here are some other forms of meditation that I found

- **Mindfulness Meditation:** The most well-known type of meditation, mindfulness meditation, is about being aware of the sounds and activities happening around you. It's almost a flow-like type of meditation, because you literally just let your mind be fluid and flow from one thought to the next, not really focusing on one particular thing. For instance, if you live in a noisy city, you don't have to block out the outside sirens and screaming children, you let your mind be aware of the sounds without becoming too focused.

- **Spiritual Meditation** This type of meditation is for those who regularly participate in prayer, as it's based on communicating with God. Just like the other styles, you must become calm and quiet and then begin to focus on a question or problem you might have. This style of meditation can feel not only relaxing, but rewarding as well.

- **Focused Meditation** If the idea of clearing your mind of all thoughts stresses you out, focused meditation is great because you can focus on a sound, object, mantra, or thought. The key here is to just focus on one of these things and stay committed to that one thought or object. This is when relaxation music comes in handy. Even though you're essentially using your mind, you'll be amazed at how rejuvenated you feel afterwards. In our day to day lives, our minds really are in 10 different places at once!

- **Movement Meditation:** Movement meditation may seem intimidating, but if you're by yourself and you really get into it, it can be extremely uplifting and relaxing at the same time. Sitting with your eyes closed, simply focus on your breath and try out different gentle, repetitive flowing movements. Rather than focus on a sound, object, or thought, just turn your attention to your movement. I find a slow left and right swaying motion to be therapeutic, or you could try moving your entire upper body in a slow circular motion.

- **Mantra Meditation:** Mantras are words that are chanted loudly during meditation. It may seem odd to be making loud noises during a meditation session, but it's actually the sounds that become the object being focused on. In yoga, the mantra Om is regularly used since it delivers a deep vibration that makes it easy for the mind to concentrate on that particular sound.

Let's stay with the "For Dummies" Series -

"Meditation for Dummies"

by

Stephan Bodian

You can order this book as Paper Back or
Ebook on our website:
WWW.PTSDHotline.Com

Other helpful topics that have popped up with regards to Veterans and PTSD

- **Yoga:** The words "Department of Defense" and "yoga" aren't often uttered in the same breath, let alone in a long, conscious, exhale. But preliminary results from a small study funded by the U.S. Defense Department, and led by a Harvard Medical School assistant professor; found that veterans diagnosed with post-traumatic stress disorder showed improvement in their symptoms after ten weeks of yoga classes. This includes meditation and breathing, done twice a week, and fifteen minutes of daily practice at home.

- **Acupuncture:** Acupuncture is just now beginning to be investigated as a potential treatment for PTSD. However, findings are quite promising. Dr. Michael Hollifield and colleagues at the University of New Mexico compared acupuncture to group cognitive behavioral therapy and no treatment among a group of people who had been exposed to traumatic events and were experiencing PTSD symptoms. They found that acupuncture was just as effective as group cognitive behavioral therapy and more effective than no treatment in reducing PTSD symptoms, depression, anxiety, and life impairment. They also found that these reductions persisted over a three-month period..

More on these subjects can be found on our message boards at:

WWW.PTSDHotline.Com

Chapter 7
Physical Health
Body Heal Thyself!

What's in this Chapter?

Some of this chapter will sound like rants against things that actually should upset all of us anyway:

- The Fast Food Industry
- Doctors, Insurance Companies and Psychiatrists as Pill Pushers!
- Medical Schools: What sells!!!
- Negative Thinking and its Money Making Machine

I'll try to play nice but even as I do rewrites on this chapter I can feel my blood pressure creeping up on me. Some of this info will send me flying back into my Anger Management classes! Is ranting negative thinking? That is really open to interpretation. When is Ranting healthy? Just what I need!

Something else to get positive or negative about! The push and pull, Yin and Yang of it all!

I will give you **Rant Alerts** along the way☺

Integrative Medicine

To balance out any rants below it is important for me to talk about the future of medicine. More and more doctors are looking at holistic medicine to add to their little black bag of tricks. Doctors no longer need to rely solely on toxic drugs.

Many Americans have never heard of integrative medicine, but this holistic movement has left its imprint on many of the nation's hospitals, universities, and medical schools.

Holistic Medicine is practiced much more in other parts of the world.

Treating the Whole Person

Both doctors and patients alike are bonding with the philosophy of Integrative Medicine and its whole-person approach which is designed to treat the person, not just the disease.

I.M., as it's often called, depends on a partnership between the patient and the doctor. The goal is to treat the mind, body, and spirit, all at the same time.

While some of the therapies used may be non-conventional, a guiding principle within Integrative Medicine is to use therapies that have some high-quality evidence to support them.

Conventional and Alternative Approaches

The Duke Center for Integrative Medicine is a classic model of Integrative Medicine. It combines conventional Western medicine with alternative or complementary treatments, such as herbal medicine, acupuncture, massage, biofeedback, yoga, and stress reduction techniques -- all in the effort to treat the whole person. Proponents prefer the term "complementary" to emphasize that such treatments are used with mainstream medicine, not as replacements or alternatives, but as additional therapy to enhance their benefits. The combination is not a reduction but a synergy to boost the results.

Integrative medicine got a boost of greater public awareness -- and funding -- after a landmark 1993 study. That study showed that one in three Americans had used an alternative therapy, often under the medical radar.

Legal Statement It is important for me to say, at the beginning of this chapter on health, to follow the advice of your doctor, psychiatrist, psychologist, etc. There are many times when drugs are necessary at least on a short term basis. Don't be afraid to get a second opinion. You can eliminate drugs later by becoming proactive in your body's ability to heal itself.

Here we go:

You have made it to another step!. You are going to PTSD Program meetings and gaining important information from the other vets that you are now associating with. Talk about Yin and Yang. We vets can be a real mixed bag! It is important to learn how to farm the "Wheat from the Chaff"! The important thing to remember is that there is a ton of great info in the ocean of knowledge we Vets contain. Just don't take everything to the bank!

Hopefully you are now even receiving monthly financial help for your service connected issues. You have come a long way. You are now using **Self-Hypnosis, Meditation** and have joined a pot smoking commune.

Oops! Hopefully my book hasn't sent you that far down the garden path. We are not lemmings!!! Don't get on the Flower Power Buss and head over the nearest cliff! You Vietnam Era vets will get a kick out of this:

Positive Steps:

Things are really looking up. You are making positive steps in the right direction. That alone should give you a feeling of power over what you want to get out of life. You no longer allow life to push you around like a feather in a dust storm. The longer you exert your control in a positive way the easier it becomes. Others may see these positive changes in your life before you do. Once you see your life improving in even a small way take heart from it and use the affirmation to realize that you can indeed take control and grab your life back.

Take this time to appreciate that you have taken important steps toward becoming a:

War Zone PTSD Survivor!

What was next for me?

When the above began happening for me it was the turning point in my life. There were still some downward spirals ahead but they became much easier to stop and deal with. It became easier and easier to get back on track.

Regaining the control over my life opened up a lot of time. "Wasted days and Wasted Nights" was a song from those times. This was time I had been wasting on self-medication and the lengthy hangovers that this caused.

With that extra clarity of mind I could now concentrate on other issues that I had been being lax with. My body needed some work!

My Physical Wellbeing!
Healing My Body
Diet, Exercise, & Positive Thinking!

Once I got to this stage, in my recovery, I started asking myself why I didn't feel physically better! Why didn't I feel super healthy? I had cut out the self-medications. Shouldn't I wake up in the morning feeling refreshed and raring to go?

Could it be that I was 70 pounds overweight and taking blood pressure and cholesterol drugs?

Rant Alert! But aren't those legal drugs prescribed by my doctor? Didn't he give them to me to make me healthy?

I was studying and working hard to eliminate negative thinking and bad substances from my life and here I was still taking drugs. They may have been legal drugs and doctors may have been prescribing them to me but in my mind they are the same as the illegal poison drug cartels push. The line between legal and illegal drugs is hazy at best. They are both toxic and extremely dangerous.

Between my Service Connected Benefits and our SSI we were now receiving a decent income. I still felt like there was something missing. There is no amount of financial security that makes up for poor health. Plus you can't make continuing good decisions about your future if your body is all out of whack! Your brain just doesn't function properly.

Had I gone through all this psychological healing work to die at an early age from high blood pressure, cholesterol or some other physical health issues? *No way!*

I started thinking: *I have come so far. I have taken back control of my anger and other PTSD issues.*

What do I need to do to get healthy? What's next?" (Positive Question)

I started looking at it positively. Wouldn't it be fun to pull on a pair of pants without yanking and wiggling around like Houdini in his straight jacket? I knew what I needed to do.

I would spin the clock backwards!

My time capsule would be in the form of gel caps full of the vitamins and nutrients that had been missing in my life. My time machine would be in the form of a bicycle and stair stepper.

I remember how good I felt waking up every morning when I was young. Back then I couldn't wait to get moving. There was a whole world of adventure out there!

Note: Notice the Internal conversations and questions I was asking myself? They were all addressed in a positive form!

Before I learned how to deal with PTSD my personal questions would have been negatively stated like this:

- What the hell is wrong with me?
- Why am I such a screw up?
- How did I get so fat?
- How could I be so stupid?

One of the best things you can do for yourself and everyone else around you is to retrain your mind to "**Ask yourself positive questions.**" Write or type this out

Positive questions put positive actions into motion!

Print out this positive statement and tape it on the ceiling above your bed. It will be the first thing you read every morning.

The reverse of this is also true! Negative thoughts are very harmful. Let's call them ANTs!

ANTs:

Negative questions and thoughts reinforce the bad habits in our life! The **ANTs** are really sneaky. What are ANTs? **Automatic Negative Thoughts!**

Example My wife and I started talking about our progress. I had lost a little more weight than she had. She said that she had heard that men lose weight faster than women. That is how sneaky ANTs can be.

Men and women do lose weight at different rates. However you have to be careful not to allow your mind to latch onto thoughts like this to use as an excuse. Just that simple little ANT could cause her metabolism to slow down. That sounds simplistic but it is true. Can you imagine what ANTs like "I will always be fat!" or "I am a failure" can cause?

Kill All Ants! Remember the brain is your body's conductor. Give it only positive sheet music!

Also it was important for me to remind both Ginger and myself that this was not a race.

This was not a diet but a way of living a healthier lifestyle for the rest of our lives. Acting like it's a race can allow all types of negative reactions into the equation. Any small setback can then derail the whole train.

Note: I want to really thank Dr Daniel Amen for the use of his acronym ANTs. Automatic Negative Thoughts. His statement "Kill All ANTs" really helps me. Anytime an ANT pops into my mind now I spot it right away and laugh at it. Look Dr Daniel Amen up on the internet or check out one of his PBS Specials. Interesting stuff!

Author's Note: Here is something I heard from Doctor Oz that I like: Use the **"80 X 20 Rule"**.

To become successful at improving your life don't stick yourself with the impossible task of being 100% perfect. Do not let some 20% walks on "The Wild Side" turn your life back into a downward spiral. I have been considered a War Zone PTSD Survivor for a number of years now and I am still shooting for the **90% x**

10% to happen in my life. Living a **"real life"** allows me to live with some realistic goals.

Use It Or Lose It!
Also Pertains to the Muscle in your Head!

There are so many great things to study and research regarding your brain and body. Just the act of learning these new things is much more important than you may realize. *"Stretching the Mind"* is not just one of those things said in conversation. The elasticity of the brain's ability to learn makes this statement extremely important to you. It is as important as stretching all of the other physical muscles in your body. People that lead a sedentary lifestyle never studying new information or working their imagination allow their brains to atrophy. This causes really bad things like early onset Alzheimer's

Starting the Day off with a smile

OK after you open your eyes in the morning and you have read your ceiling☺, take the time to relax in the warmth of your bed for a few extra minutes meditating on your happy list. Mine involves thinking about my grandkids and other fun things in my life. This starts me out every day with a smile. This is really easy to do and it can affect the course of your whole day.

Here's another great idea. Write out a list of positive actions that you want to draw into your own life.

Example of my list:

- Eat a healthy *__diet__ to power up my brain
- Reach and maintain my ideal weight
- Enjoy a wonderful sex life with my wife (I really like this one. Now I just have to   convince her!)
- Spend quality time with my kids and grandkids
- Help as many veterans as I can

Place your list somewhere handy so that you can meditate on it every morning. Every list like this should have something that improves someone else's life. Random acts of kindness can improve your own health and wellbeing more than many other things you can do.

Note: Many people misuse and mistrust the word *__diet__. I don't use it as it relates to weight loss. Many people that have used things like "YoYo Dieting" view the word diet in an extremely negative light. Losing or gaining weight depending on what your body needs is just an automatic benefit of living a healthy lifestyle. I use the word **diet** strictly to reference everything that I eat, drink or put into my body to stay alive. We have to call it something. For instance my diet does not include ingesting drugs, cigarettes, too much alcohol, or caffeine. As I have already stated the word diet relates to what I ingest to keep me alive not to make me dead!

Negative Thoughts – ANTs

Don't pay attention to every negative thought that pops into your mind! Just because it pops into your head doesn't make it true.

Have you ever been sitting in church or some public place and a really creepy thought pops up out of nowhere? At least in church you can blame the thought on El Diablo. You know he hates seeing you sitting there with a nice smile on your face. You can always jump up and scream as loud as you can; **"Get behind me Satan!"** The people in the pew behind you may take exception to that though. They don't want that negative thought in their row either. Your pastor, priest or rabbi may not be too happy with you either. The best thing to do is just pay no attention to those intruding little buggers.

Learning how to **"Kill all Ants"** and asking yourself positive constructive questions is a major step in the right direction. No one likes being around negative people. It really is unhealthy and it rubs off on everyone around you especially yourself.

Negative Thoughts show up in more than just your brain!

Can negative thoughts mess with your physical body? Does the brain have **anything** to

do with your physical health? No not anything.
Everything!

When you get embarrassed doesn't your
face turn red? Your skin is one of the major
organs of the body. That little skin reaction to
something in your head should prove to you
that your brain is the conductor of the whole
symphony orchestra that is you body. The body
has billions upon billions of musicians (cells) to
deal with. The brain is a busy boy or girl. Those
ANTS are like sour notes blaring out of the
trumpet section. Hearing the sour note causes
another musician to accidentally drop the
cymbals! All hell breaks loose.

Am I over reacting to Automatic
Negative Thoughts? No I'm not. Those ANTS
will disrupt the Rhythm of your Brain and the
Symphony starts to lose direction!!! Give your
conductor (brain) a big break. Stay Positive My
Friends!

Are all negative thoughts a disaster?
Only if you make them so. I use humor to keep
my ANT's at bay. I attribute negative thoughts
to dumb jokes my mind is trying to pull over on

me. I just laugh at them. I give them **"No Respect"** as Rodney Dangerfield would say!

Physical Healing became my next target on my road to recovery!

Looking back I can now see how my life took such a drastic turn toward the dark side. PTSD issues pushed me into years of self-medication with illegal drugs and alcohol. This is the Mother of all Slippery Slopes! Once I took that nasty turn I was hooked for many more years than I care to remember. Actually I don't remember many of the things that went on during those dark times.

Did I know better? Absolutely!

Did I care? I must not have cared enough because it consumed many years of my life. The sad part is that it affected the lives of the people around me!

This is the ugly underbelly of what PTSD causes our young men and women coming back from war. It ruins the lives of our warriors and their family and friends as well. Many veterans don't come back from this slide into horrible Physical and Mental Disease. It leads to suicide and early death.

Veteran Suicides!

This may be a good time to discuss suicide as if there is ever anything good to say about it. This chapter is about Health and Physical Wellbeing. Would it surprise you to learn that suicide can be directly related to your diet?

Here is an article I just read in Parade (July 4th 2012), a mini magazine insert in many local newspapers.

Mood-Boosting Super Foods
Fatty Fish

More than half the human brain is composed of fat, and two types seem to be crucial to mood: the omega-3 fats DHA and EPA, found in fish such as salmon and mackerel. Last year scientists analyzed the blood of U.S. veterans who had **committed suicide** and found lower levels of DHA than were found in veterans who reported no suicidal feelings.

And in 2011, a research review by the New York State Psychiatric Institute concluded that EPA can significantly reduce the symptoms of depression.

Happiness Boosting Rx At least two servings of seafood especially fatty fish, each week.

Tomatoes

The molecules that give this fruit its characteristic red, orange, or yellow hue are carotenoids, antioxidants that counteract the damage of free radicals, which destroy mood protecting fats in the brain.

A 2011 study from the National Institute on Aging found that older people who filled up on carotenoid –rich foods were 28 percent less likely to be depressed. Also "people with high blood levels of carotinoids have lower rates of memory loss and dementia", says Drew Ramsey, MD., a Columbia University psychiatrist specializing in nutrition and co-author of the Happiness Diet.

Happiness-Boosting Rx One serving (about a cup) of tomatoes per day-either fresh or in tomato based sauces or low sugar ketchup or salsa.

Whole Grains

Noshing on carbs promotes the release of insulin, a hormone that stimulates serotonin production. To avoid a blood sugar spike choose whole grains not processed grains of any kind. Don't eat carbs and proteins together; doing so can block the effects of serotonin.

Mixing proteins and carbs can cause all sorts of problems with digestion problems including slowing down the metabolism.

Author's Note: For more information on mixing proteins, carbs and food combining read Harvey Diamonds books mentioned at the bottom of this chapter. He is an expert on food combining for health!

Happiness Boasting Rx Two cups of air popped popcorn or whole grain graham crackers

Spinach

These leafy greens are loaded with Folate - a B vitamin the brain uses to make several mood-regulating chemicals including serotonin, dopamine, and norepinephrine. Other folate-packed foods include lentils and asparagus.

Up to 50% of people with depression are folate-deficient. A 2010 report from the American Psychiatric Assoc. even noted that folate may be effective in treating depression!

Happiness Boosting Rx One to two cups of spinach, or other folate-rich foods per day.

Folate: What is it? (From the office of Dietary Supplements)

Folate is a water-soluble B vitamin that occurs naturally in food. Folic acid is the synthetic form of folate that is found in supplements and added to fortified foods.

Folate gets its name from the Latin word "folium" for leaf. A key observation of researcher Lucy Wills nearly 70 years ago led to the identification of folate as the nutrient needed to prevent the anemia of pregnancy. Dr. Wills demonstrated that the anemia could be corrected by a yeast extract. Folate was identified as the corrective substance in yeast extract in the late 1930s, and was extracted from spinach leaves in 1941.

Folate helps produce and maintain new cells [2]. This is especially important during periods of rapid cell division and growth such as infancy and pregnancy. Folate is needed to make DNA and RNA, the building blocks of cells. It also helps prevent changes to DNA that may lead to cancer [3]. Both adults and children need folate to make normal red blood cells and prevent anemia [4]. Folate is also essential for the metabolism of homocysteine, and helps maintain normal levels of this amino acid.

Dark Chocolate:☺ Authors Note: There must be something to chocolate. It puts a smile on my face just typing the word! **AHHHH – Chocolate!**

Chocolate-particularly the dark kind, which by definition consists of at least 60 percent cocoa-is thought to increase the brains serotonin levels.

Chocolate may also increase mental alertness. In a 2010 study, British researchers asked 300 people to drink cocoa drinks or similar-tasting cocoa-free drinks and then gave them a series of cognitive tasks, like solving arithmetic problems. Those that drank the cocoa performed significantly better and felt less mentally drained afterward.

Happiness Boasting Rx One ounce of dark chocolate daily.

Authors note I would probably screw up my blood pressure trying to stop at just one ounce☺.

Authors Note: This last one below I reluctantly put in here. I need to be fair to the whole article from Parade so I added it. I am not trying to turn anyone into a vegetarian. I am not one myself. I love fish and chicken. I will have a juicy steak once every couple of months. The problems occur when people eat red meat with abandon in large quantities. Too much of anything is not good and red meat really falls into the category of careful moderation.

Red Meat

We know! We know! Red meat has its detractors. But it's an incredibly good source of iron, which the brain needs to make mood regulating chemicals like dopamine; in fact people that are iron deficient may be 50% more susceptible to depression than those with higher levels.

Meat from grass feed cows contains more happiness promoting omega-3 fats (The good kind) than beef from conventionally raised cows. Stick to lean, unprocessed cuts-more roast beef than hot dogs.

Vegetarian meat substitutes Though it is harder to absorb iron from non-meat sources the best bets are beans, dried fruits, and whole grains.

Happiness Boosting Rx Two small servings of red meat each week- a total of 8 to 12 ounces.

You do not have to eat meat to get iron into your diet!

The body needs oxygen for survival and iron is the primary nutrient in charge of delivering it to all of the body's cells, tissues and organs. Low iron stores result in fatigue, poor concentration, irritability -- symptoms of a condition called iron deficiency anemia.

Below is Info on iron deficiency emailed to me by Harvey Diamond author of the #1 Best Selling Health Book **"Fit For Life":**

Hi Don;

As per your question regarding iron deficiency:

Generally speaking anything green and leafy is going to have iron in it and the darker the better like spinach and kale. Broccoli is also a good source. Most seeds (ideally raw) are great sources - sesame, sunflower, and pumpkin. Also most nuts (ideally raw), particularly almonds and cashews are great. Dried fruit (naturally dried is best) is very good – especially figs, raisins, apricots, and prunes. Also most berries especially blueberries, raspberries, and strawberries. Peas, most all beans especially lima beans, and lentils and chickpeas, are high in iron as well.

Honestly I have stopped trying to convince traditionally trained dietitians, nutritionists, and M.D.s of anything—far too many are stuck in the past when it comes to diet and nutrition. They are, all too often, in a corrupt relationship with the dairy and animal products industries.

They ignorantly try to convince people that being healthy and obtaining certain nutrients like iron, or protein, calcium, Vitamin B, omegas, and a host of others is only possible by eating dead animals, or animal products such as dairy. As if the Grand Creator worked things out in such a way that the only means by which we can survive and obtain what we need to remain healthy is by slaughtering and consuming other sentient beings on our planet.

All it takes is a little common sense to realize that the animals we supposedly have to eat in order to obtain nutrients ate plant foods to build those nutrients in the first place. But tragically, that obvious, intelligent argument is wasted on those who have been educated beyond their intelligence and therefore know a whole lot about what is not so.

"Beware of false knowledge; it is more dangerous than ignorance." –George Bernard Shaw

More Common Sense Statements
The 10% Rule

Don't stress out about your health and diet! Don't try to do it all at once as you will more than likely fall short and feel like you failed. This can lead to a downward spiral.

Adding 10% more exercise and 10% less junk food is easy and will lead to jump starting your healthy new lifestyle

Here is another Easy way to get started:

Meatless Mondays

Meatless Monday is an international campaign that encourages people to not eat meat on Mondays to improve their health and the health of the planet.

Going meatless once a week may reduce your risk of chronic preventable conditions like cancer, cardiovascular disease, diabetes and obesity. It can also help reduce your carbon footprint and save precious resources like fresh water and fossil fuel.

Benefits of Good Nutrition

Rant Alert: Without good nutrition you cannot expect your brain to function in your best interest. You know this. Everyone knows this. It is so obvious and yet take a look at the long lines of cars waiting at the takeout windows of the local poison palaces. The people won't even get off their butts to walk inside.

That is OK. The 20 odd steps of exercise won't help digest the *"Butt Burger in a Bag"* that is waiting inside for them.

After forcing this crap down their throats they then drive back to work wondering why they would much rather pull over and take a nap!

Smile & Say Cheese!

How would you like to look into the camera and see this picture of yourself?

I am speaking from many long unhealthy years of experience?

Throw a couple of arms and legs on that butt burger above and there I was. I looked like the Poster Boy for a Buffet Line! I changed the statement:

"All You Can Eat" to "Eat Yourself Sick!"

Eating yourself sick is exactly what most people do their whole lives and then wonder what happened when their doctor lays the bad news on them. "You're sick but relax we have drugs for that!"☺

I call these poisonous conglomerations in the photo above, **Butt Burgers**. Guess where they end up? On your **BUTTTTTTT!** People then wonder why their bodies are shaped like a pear!

This stupidity happened to me and I really should have known better. I studied health along with my family back in the 1980's. I actually know a lot more about the subject of Health and Prevention than the average person. I know more about prevention than most practicing medical doctors as well. Most medical schools do not teach even a single one hour class on prevention at all.

Fit For Life

My family helped put on large Health Seminars for Harvey Diamond who wrote the fastest selling Health books of all time – **"Fit For Life"**. Over 12 million copies in print!

"Fit For Life" has been in print since the mid 1980's and still sells 50,000 copies a year!

Harvey is a world renowned healer. His 40+ years of studying the human body and how it works has helped many thousands of people all over the world achieve optimum health.

If I could become this out of whack with my background in the study of Physical Health then it could happen to anyone!

More on Harvey the Vietnam Vet later in this chapter.

The Power of Positive Thinking

I actually understood the physical and psychological benefits of staying positive as well.

One of the people we were working with back then, to put on these seminars, was a young unknown man named Anthony Robbins. Yes that Tony Robbins. Tony was a lot of fun to work with and had an incredible sense of humor. Talk about a human dynamo. What he has done since those early days is mind boggling. I remembered Tony as an extreme positive thinker.

Even with all my studies of physical health and positive thinking I wasn't able to take advantage of it in my own life. Back then I did not understand just how deeply my mental problems, caused by my war experiences and the aftermath, were. As I have said before in this guide the VA of the 1980's still did not have a grasp on just what was wrong with all the returning veterans. No one had yet heard the acronym PTSD!

21st Century!

Now here I was in the 21st Century. Did I have PTSD? Yes I now understood that full well. I was making large strides in my understanding of what I needed to do to live a better life.

PTSD is an extremely negative condition!

One of the things that I needed to do next was to stop dwelling on the negative. I needed to latch back onto the Positive Thinking and the Physical Healing principles that I had set aside on my mad rush to the liquor stores and the drug dealers of the world.

For years I had buried a powerful basic understanding of the principles of **"Body Heal**

Thyself!" Now that I knew what PTSD was and what it was doing to me I could say *"No!"* to it and grab my life back out of the darkness.

A Healthy Family

All I had to do was take a look at my own family to know that I too could be super healthy.

My mom and sister still follow Harvey's health principles today and are in fantastic condition. My mom, until very recently, traveled all over the West going to County Fairs in Clog Dancing Troupes. **She is 87!** The only thing that has temporarily slowed her down is a recent knee replacement surgery. The doctors could not believe that she was doing so incredibly well with this operation at her age. She is now like a race horse in the starting gate. She can't wait to get moving again.

My sister Marcia is the original Energizer Bunny. She is 65. She is married to a wonderful tall strapping guy named Thor. He is 15 years her junior. She would run right over a husband her own age. If you ever met her you would swear that she is in her 40's.

My brother Steve who is in his 60's outworks the 20 year old laborers he hires for his landscape and construction business. He works out every morning before he heads out to do serious labor.

My youngest brother Bill is also in his 60's and was on Chuck Norris's Exhibition Karate Team. He still out pedals anyone he is with going up and down steep mountains on his Mountain Bike several times a week.

What the hell happened to me? I know that sounds like an **ANT** type question, but in this instance I used it for positive action. Could too many years of hard living through the miracle of drug therapy have gotten in my way? We vets call it Self-Medication. Doctors call it drug therapy. I now call it **Just Plain Stupid** on both counts!

More Rant Alert! Of course the VA did its share of enabling me along the way. As I have said in this guide the VA in the past had a drug or ten for all occasions.

I had been on blood pressure meds, from the VA, for years. I decided to get my health back on track and losing weight was an important start. Guess what? My blood pressure immediately dropped accordingly. What a big whoop whoop surprise☺!

I kept telling my doctor, at the VA, that I wanted to stop taking the blood pressure drugs he had me on. He looked at me like I was nuts.

Finally after self-monitoring my BP for a month I decided to dump the drugs. About three months later I went in for a regular checkup with my doc. He checked my BP and was really happy with it. He had a smug look on his face like **"Look what I have done for you!"**

I then told him that I had stopped taking the pills months ago. His smile crumbled. He got really agitated and his eyes started spinning in circles like pinwheels. Sweat popped out all over his forehead. He damn near ripped my arm off trying to do another BP test! This time I tested even better than the first test!

In a state of denial he finally said, **"OK we will keep monitoring you."** It should have made him happy for me but instead he just shook his head. Doctors are trained in Drug Therapy for everything. They are not trained in prevention. They only get involved once you are sick.

They could make a great living helping people remain healthy before the fact through teaching prevention and selling vitamins and supplements. Unfortunately they are part of the trillion dollar money machine that the Drug Industry brings in. There's gold in **Them Thar' Toxic Hills of Pills.**

Author's Note: The above is an over dramatization of what actually happened with my VA doctor but it was fun to write. He did over react a little to the situation though. His eyes didn't actually spin! He is a really nice guy and a good doctor.

Are the blood pressure meds toxic? Of course they are! Don't let anyone fool you, **All Drugs Are Toxic!** They all have bad side effects and many of them are extremely dangerous to your life even when taken according to the directions.

Listen to the commercials with the insane lists of side effects that they try to hide with some pleasant background music. It is amazing how they think that the right soothing song can mask a statement like, *<u>"May cause irritable bowel syndrome!"</u>*

They should follow that up with, "But wait we have a drug for your inflamed bowels as well!" They could then do another litany of the side effects of that drug. They could then say again; "**But Wait!**" and on and on it could go! Finally someone has invented the *Perpetual Money Machine!* Oops, I meant Perpetual *Motion* Machine!

Pain Pills

Just because drugs mask some of the pain they have nothing to do with healing the problems that caused the pain in the first place. Drugs do not heal! In the case of my blood pressure they allowed me to stay fat. I could keep eating junk food☺! I did not have to lose weight to lower my BP. How fun is that? So what if my weight was ruining other parts of my body. So what if the BP Meds would cause other problems over the long haul!

On top of that the drugs added more bad toxins to a beautiful healing machine which is the body. The body works 24/7 to eliminate toxins to allow you to actually heal naturally. The important keyword here is **HEAL!** Why screw that up by throwing a bunch of toxic crap back down your throat?

But don't drugs help with pain? In many cases they do mask some of the pain. But is this always the smart thing to do?

Pain is a natural function of your body's safety and healing processes. It warns you that there is something wrong and that you should pull your hand out of the blazing hot fire. Masking that pain is really dangerous. Hiding from the cause of the pain could very well be deadly to you. Drugs are worse than playing Russian roulette. At least Russian roulette won't allow you to become worse and worse year after year until you eventually die. Just one wrong cylinder and BLAMO! No more suffering for you. The drug companies hate Russian roulette though. Another customer bites the dust while they still have money in their bank account. Healing puts a cramp in their bottom line.

Your body is already dealing with toxins in the air, the water that you drink and many of the foods that you eat. Every day your body has to remove millions of dead and toxic cells that have completed their life cycle. They need to go bye bye. Why give it more to do? With all that work it is no wonder so many people feel tired all the time.

Now don't misunderstand me. If I was in a car wreck and had bad injuries I would be at the front of the Pain Killer queue!

The Health Machine

Don't confuse your body's healing machine by adding junk like legal or illegal drugs that are toxic and are also really dangerous and expensive on top of that. You are paying big bucks to destroy yourself. When you really think about it that way it is downright mind-blowingly stupid! There are so many natural healthy alternatives to drugs. Things that actually heal you. It is time for you to find out what they are.

Breaking News While I am sitting here typing away I just heard on the news that doctors and scientists have just reduced a type of skin cancer with a green tea extract that caused no side effects!

I could go on and on about healthy eating and exercise. I am thrilled to be back with Harvey Diamond again. His book "Fit For Life – A New Beginning" is a must read for you:

http://www.HarveyDiamond.com/

I trust Harvey because over the past 25 years that I have known him I have seen his health principles work wonders in my own family. I got side tracked but guess what? It is not too late for me and it is not too late for you either. Plus Harvey is a Vet. I trust Vets.

Vets Helping Vets!

Harvey Diamond the Vietnam Vet and Agent Orange

Here is another reason to trust Harvey's extensive knowledge of health. He has a personal history with Agent Orange! His personal battle with Agent Orange is an amazing story in itself. He continues to heal himself, without drugs, from a debilitating illness caused by the Agent Orange he was doused with in Vietnam.

He has lived for many years' totally drug free and without pain from the Agent Orange Induced Peripheral Neuropathy he has lived with the past 25 years. He was told that he would be in a wheel chair or dead within 5 years from the time he first realized he had it. We are talking 25 years ago and he is still writing books and will continue to do so for many years to come. The people who were giving him the death sentence and were dealing with their own Agent Orange death sentence including Peripheral Neuropathy are all dead now. They all died 25 years ago. I just talked to Harvey on the phone and he sure seemed quite alive to me. In fact he was all excited about his new book coming out soon.

What is Peripheral Neuropathy?

Damage to the peripheral nervous system interrupts communication between the brain and other parts of the body. This can impair muscle movement, prevent normal sensation in the hands and feet, and cause different feelings including numbness, tingling, cold and excruciating pain.

Rant Alert!

Doctors are mystified as to how it is possible that someone dealing with what Harvey has is still living **Pain Free** without drugs. The fact that he can walk at all defies what doctors believe he should be able to do without their mountains of drugs. He has never taken drugs of any kind! By the way all their drugs are not helping the many other vets that are living with horrible pain from Peripheral Neuropathy thanks to Agent Orange. Well not actually living with it. Most of the ones that contracted what Harvey has back then from Agent Orange in Vietnam are dead! Yes DEAD! I can't express this strongly enough! Harvey is living and walking proof that his health principles work and work extremely well!

Here is another one of the lovely little Catch 22's that must have been **Hatched in Hell.** Agent Orange percolates in the body for many, many years. As in Harvey's case it did not manifest itself into things like Peripheral Neuropathy for 20 years or more after he was doused.

How do you ask for help and benefits from the VA for something you didn't even know that you had? How do you get the VA to acknowledge your condition as Service Connected 20 years after the fact? They do know that he has it and they do know he got it from Agent Orange or some type of orange. I guess they figure he must have picked it up having lived in Orange County, California for years. The tie in of Orange must have been enough for them to deny him his benefits. Some reasons they give for denying vets their benefits is mystifying to the max unless you have a cynical mind like mine!

This is serious stuff my fellow Vets and it makes me want to scream at the sky! Does Harvey have Service Connected Benefits? As of this writing - **NO!** Will he ever get them? Probably not!

Besides he should be dead by now like the rest of those Agent Orange Vets that got things like Peripheral Neuropathy.

Harvey's 40 years of brilliant research in preventing illness through Natural Hygiene, nutrition and cleansing the body of all the toxins bombarding us daily allows him to live pain free. He has a limp while walking and some other physical issues like trying to get a glass of drinking water to his lips. This is due to what Agent Orange has caused him. The fact that he is still able to drink water at all speaks volumes!

You may ask if Harvey was so healthy then why Agent Orange has affected him at all. That would be like thinking that you are so healthy what harm could sticking your arm into a bubbling vat of acid do? Agent Orange is dioxin! The most deadly chemical toxin ever designed by man.

Think about the vets that don't have Harvey's knowledge and don't live a healthy lifestyle that is constantly helping the body heal itself. These Vets are either dead or in deep trouble.

Would you consider Harvey a Walking Miracle? No actually it is not a miracle! He began his **walk** with health 20 years before he knew he had Agent Orange in his system. He is able to still walk and live pain free because he is a **Walking Encyclopedia** of healthy living no matter what storms life has thrown at him.

When I decided to get physically healthy again Harvey's name jumped into my mind first due to our past association. I went online at Harvey's website and bought his book "Fit For Life – A New Beginning" at full price. It didn't even hurt my pocket book. A whopping $7.44 plus shipping! About $15.00 total. What blew me away was that it also came with a bunch of other CD's, DVD's etc. This is the deal of the century! Under $20.00 that could save this many lives really is the **Deal of the Century**.

After reading this book I reached out to Harvey and he got back to me. We are now in communication and I am enjoying picking his amazing brain. This guy does not just talk the talk. He really lives his health principles. He walks the walk especially after he was told he would be in a wheel chair or worse 25 years ago. Welcome Home Brother!

It is time to help your body heal itself!

My guide, which you are reading can really help you Survive PTSD issues. For the rest of your body order Harvey's:

"Fit For Life – A New Beginning"
Today!!!

You can type this into your browser: http://tinyurl.com/7tk4z8q

Now please keep in mind that I make nothing for recommending Harvey's books. I believe in his health principles and I always support the work of my Fellow Vets.

"Vets Helping Vets"

It makes me really happy to help pass the word on Harvey's books. These books will give you a strong background in everything you will need to do to become super healthy for the rest of your life.

My wife and I now follow Harvey's Health Principles 100% and I actually wake up every morning feeling like a kid again. Today July 10th 2012 is my 67th Birthday. Talking about how great I now feel every morning when I wake up is just thrilling to me!

Is Living a Healthy life a big chore?

I don't want to place anything else on you that will make you nervous. Living with PTSD has given you enough to worry about as it is. In fact digging in and realizing that you can actually get your health back is extremely liberating.

If you wake up tomorrow being totally bummed out about that deep fried Twinkie you had at the County Fair you don't have to freak out. With the right tools it is easy to reverse it today.

I live with a default eating plan that I really enjoy. That makes it easy to bounce right back to it. As I mentioned it is my birthday today. I am going out with my family to a great local Mexican restaurant. There is not much on their menu that fits into my default eating plan. I am looking forward to the restaurant because I know that going there will not cause me any big downward spiral into days of gorging on burritos smothered in beans and melted cheese.

Until you get stronger with your eating plan I don't recommend hanging out at your favorite pizza joint every night. That is where using common sense makes it so much easier to become healthy.

It is easy to get healthy once you have the type of basic knowledge that I now live my life by. It really is not that complex at all. Becoming healthy does not require a life time of study. Once you start you will be surprised at just how common sense the information is.

Let's do a little common sense health test:

- Are deep fried foods like French fries good for you? _____
- Do you notice any change in your kids' behavior when they eat sugar laden things like
- Doughnuts or candy bars? _____
- Does drinking too much alcohol make you feel bad the next morning? ____
- Do drugs have bad side effects? _____
- Should you drink water from the manmade lake at your local park? ____

I know these are ridiculously simple questions above. Well I damn sure hope for your sake that they are easy ones for you to answer!

Then why do people put these ridiculously dumb things above into their body day in and day out? You say, "Well Don, I don't drink water out of the lake at the park. I saw dirty diapers floating in it the other day!"

Much of the water that you drink is actually almost that bad. Buying a good water purification unit for your home is really a great idea.

Even things like the Britta Water Filter pitcher that you see in most stores can really help.

For more info on your Physical Health ask your questions on our Message Boards at PTSDHoline.Com

Author's Note: This chapter has a number of topics that I feel very strongly about. It may come across aggressively. I actually have toned it way down through rewrites. Feel free to come on the message boards and tell me to lighten up☺

As I have said I am still around 30 lbs. over weight. I will always be a work in progress. The information in this chapter just gives me much better choices to live by.

Chapter 8

The Wrap Up

Wow! Here we are already at the end of this guide. You now have total control of your PTSD and Substance Abuse Problems. You have filed a claim for Service Connected Benefits. You are receiving benefits. Life is great! **We're done!**

Holy ***&#@%#@***!
!!!Screeching Brakes!!!

Now let's get back to reality! You are a work in progress. I am a work in progress. We will always be a work in progress. That is OK. I can live with that. None of us will ever be perfect! Trying to maintain perfect would be a royal pain in the butt! That would be way too much pressure.

Smoothing Out the Wrinkles

Living with PTSD is a rough road to travel. At first I needed a giant steam roller to try to smooth out the rough spots.

My life with PTSD is now more like one of those carnival games where those funny looking gopher heads pop up out of holes in the road. You have to pound them back down. Instead of a steam roller I now only need a rubber mallet to wop the problems back into their holes. I may not get a kewpie doll but living a much safer and healthier life is the greatest prize of them all.

I will always have problems but I have gained the tools to quickly smooth the road back out rather than have the problems turn into out of control downward spirals as they did in the bad old days.

Staying Consistent

Something that really helps me stay grounded is being consistent. By that I mean a default daily schedule. In the bad old days I had no schedule what so ever. My thinking patterns and my life were sporadically scattered all over the place. I never knew what was next and so basically nothing worthwhile was ever fully accomplished. I may have gotten two chapters of this guide partially completed and then I would have been off to the next great idea. I have a whole bunch of those ideas stuck in drawers. Some were good. Guess what? Now that I can plan my moves I can revisit the better ones.

Let's take a look at my favorite default type of a day:

- Wake up happy after a good 8 hours sleep. Waking up happy is easy if you have a small ritual. When I wake up I think about my granddaughters Hailey and Hensley (Puff) and a litany of only the good things in my life. Bad thoughts are not permitted! I treat this as my personal meditation time. Note: I didn't get into meditation very much in this guide but we are adding it to our website. Meditation is a great grounding tool.

- A healthy breakfast is essential. My favorite is a fruit smoothie. We have a good one. Here is a good recipe for 2 to 4 people:
- 1 or 2-cups Fresh squeezed orange juice (Not from concentrate)
- 1 or 2 Frozen Banana
- 8 or so Frozen Strawberries
- 1 whole apple – Throw in any other fresh fruit that you like
- 1 Scoop Super Food. This is 13 standard servings of dried fruits and veggies. Ask at any health foods store for a good one.
- Ice and water – Amount depends on how thick you like it.
- Note: Harvey just told me about a really great greens powder that I am going to try instead of the one I have been using. I'll let you know about it on the website.

  Blend away!
- Now it's time for my supplements: food based multi vitamin, fish oil (important). We also take a grouping of vitamin chews like D-3, 55 mg C, 250 mg Collagen, 600 mg Calcium.

- **Note:** Now that I am studying Harvey Diamond again I will use his info to design a better supplement mix that I will put into our website. He has some of the best people in the world in regards to this subject. I will have updated info on the website. The important thing for you is to get good supplements into your diet. Make sure they are food based. Make sure you get good minerals into it as well. You really need Coral Calcium in the mix. Don't buy ground up rock that some companies call minerals. Your body won't recognize them. You need minerals that have been processed through a live plants system to be the most useful to you. More on the website. Lots of info on this in Harvey's book as well.

- Work - Six or so hours of research and writing. I love to do this. If you can find some type of work that you enjoy so much the better for you. The fact that I don't work for a company allows me to break up my work time any way I like. If you can't because you are still working for a company don't worry. Just find a default day of your own that keeps you consistent. Staying consistent really helps you stay grounded.

- During the day I have 2 small healthy meals. If I get hungry I will grab a handful of raw nuts. It is surprising how good they taste after you stop craving the heavy salted type. I no longer can stand the taste of salt. If you want a salt taste try spraying the nuts with Braggs Liquid Aminos and let them dry. This is really good tasting and also very good for you. Get it at your local health food store.

- Exercise Time: Ginger and I get to the gym at Edwards Air Force Base 3 or 4 afternoons a week. It is an awesome gym and free to us. If you have a military base around you go there and arrange to get a permanent pass to get on base. Many vets can get this. Most VA Hospitals have some form of gym or exercise that you can use free.

- On days that we don't hit the gym we try to do something fun like taking our dog for a walk at the park. Chasing him as he chases the ducks actually is a lot of exercise and hysterical. Riding our bikes is also fun.

- Two more hours of research, writing, or emailing, etc.
- Supper Time: Here's a typical dinner for us:
- *5 oz Salmon – Honey Mustard Glaze Yummmmmmm. I could eat this every day. Making food a friend instead of your enemy is a total blast!
- *Large salad in a rainbow of veggie colors
- *Veggie dish: Lots of veggies like sweet peppers, yellow squash, onions, etc. I love them stir fried in a little coconut oil and sprayed while cooking with Braggs Liquid Amino's. A very light sprinkling of Spike Seasoning is OK. You can get these items at any health food store.
- **Note:** When we eat anything cooked we take enzymes. This is important. You can find out about enzymes in our website or Harvey's book.
- Kick back time: A good movie with Ginger or better yet a Dodger Game. Oops sorry about my team's plug. I do sneak a game in when I can.
- **Dessert Time!** On the days that we hit the gym I give us a super healthy evening treat. Using that Montel blender I make the most incredible frozen fruit sorbets I have ever tasted. After

having these you will never feel the need for Ben and Jerry's Wavy Gravy again. Well maybe Wavy Gravy once a year or so. Some of you are old enough to know who Wavy Gravy is. As of this writing Wavy is still alive (76 years old). Born Hugh Nanton Romney, Wavy makes the world a better place. Look him up on the internet.

- Here is one of my sorbets:
- In the Blender Add:
- 1 or 2 Frozen Banana
- Frozen Strawberries or any combo of frozen berries you like. If you buy them frozen in a bag make sure the ingredients say berries only. No sugar, no cooking nothing! No bleaching or any of the other little tricks they try to sneak by us!
- Packet Stevia - Excellent sweetener. Do not use any of those other poison packets
- Blend and if you like top with a small scoop of frozen nonfat Cool Whip.
- Sometimes I only use frozen blue berries and banana or frozen mango, fresh frozen pineapple and banana. Frozen peaches & banana is really

great. This is a fun dessert that is good for you. This is nonfat and very low in calories.

- **You will not believe how good this is!**

• Bed Time: I really enjoy reading so I will read myself to sleep with a good book about topics like Health or PTSD, etc. I will also get in some chapters of a good mystery or fantasy. I am into The Game of Thrones books right now. I now use a Kindle Fire and it is really handy. I have been going to sleep lately with Self-Hypnosis. Instead of doing the wake up countdown (count-up) I just go to sleep with positive thoughts.

Of course there are many variations to my days but the above is a comforting day for me. If I have to drive anywhere I bring my mental rubber mallet for those pesky gophers that pop up. I have a good handle on road rage now but it did take some serious mallet practice. If I run into a person in a store or somewhere else that is being obnoxious I carry an imaginary Peacock Feather to tap them on the head with.

The rubber mallet could get me into trouble. The point is to see someone acting like a clown and appreciating the humor in it. They are screwing up their day not mine!

Let's take another look at the steps you need to take Memorize these or tattoo them on your arm –

- **Get Started** – Do Something. Get out of your Comfort Zone. That cave you are hiding in will steal your life from you.
- **Vets Helping Vets** – Find out where the vets go and go there. Start Talking. Ask questions. Ask for help. What is the worst thing that could happen? You could make a friend! Vets don't turn their backs on vets! That just doesn't happen. They may get grumpy but vets don't turn their back on anyone. It is a survival tactic☺
- **Get Proactive in your Recovery** – Take the reins. This is your life. If you can't do this yourself then you must learn how to ask for help. Reaching out for help is something vets don't like to do and believe me if you don't it

will add years to your attempts to recover. Hiding will stop your recovery all together!

- **Never, Never, Never Give up on your Recovery!** The VA is there for you. Do not take no for an answer. It is just another crack so just jump it!
- **You Are Not Alone** – The problems you are dealing with are not exclusive to you. There are many thousands of veterans dealing with the exact same problems. They may have a little personal twist but basically they are the same issues.

Steps to Recovery: These all have been discussed in earlier chapters. The order can be changed to suit your situation. Don't let the size of this list bother you. This is not a race. It is your recovery! Take all the time you need once you have started the process. Don't stop the process.

- Put in the date that you start each step of the process,
- Keep track of the Doctor's, PBad or Contact Person,

- Check mark when step is completed,

  To print out this form go to :
  http://ptsdhotline.com/html/va___benefits.html
  Note: That is three underscores___ between va
  and benefits

Step		Date	Doctor or Contact	✔
1	Do a serious self-evaluation. Are you the same person you were before your war zone experience? Are you having thoughts and issues that are really disturbing? Are you having anger issues and trouble dealing with family and friends? Are you having trouble sleeping? Could you have PTSD?			
2	Come to terms with getting help. This is not wimping out unless you want to call the hundreds of thousands of vets who came before you wimps! That would not be a good idea!			
3	Go to the closest VA or Vet Center and get started. Ask about PTSD. Believe me they will know what you are asking about. Do not let a Prisoner Behind a Desk chase you off. You will recognize the vets that did not run for the hills. They are the ones with Benefits!			
4	Ask for a VA picture ID Card			
5	Fill out a Means Test and ask about Travel Pay			

6	Ask to see a VA doctor. Tell him you are having problems with PTSD. Ask for a referral to see a PTSD Doctor or Clinician			
7	Ask the doctor about getting a physical. You will need one to proceed on to the next stages.			
8	Join at least a weekly PTSD Group Meeting. If you are having problems with anger then ask about an Anger Management Program as well. If you are having Substance Abuse problems then consider AA.			
9	Find a Representative			
10	Put in a claim for Benefits.			
11	Follow up			
12	Follow Up			
13	Follow Up			
14	Make all appointments the VA sets up for you. If you can't make one you need to call to reschedule beforehand. This is important. Don't get put on anyone's back burner by being irresponsible.			
15	Keep going to meetings. This helps you stay connected to other vets which is a gas. Vets are funny and will put a smile on your face. Who else can you talk to that understands what you are dealing with from the inside out?			

16	Talk to your spouse or significant other. They are not just your caregiver. They need your support as well. What you are dealing with massively effects them too. Do not fool yourself that because they seem not interested they must be OK. They are interested but more than likely afraid to bring up the subject of what you went through! You will be surprised at how many so called caregivers have PTSD by contact with you.			
17	Re-evaluate this list often			
18	One more time altogether now one-two-three....... **Never, Never, Never give up on your recovery!!!**			

The Message Boards at:

WWW.PTSDHotline.Com

I built this website for us to use in conjunction with this Guide and to hopefully build some synergy!

Do Veterans have a voice in making changes within the VA System?

Until now the only voice most veterans have had is sitting around the VA or VFW throwing bitch sessions about all the horrors we are subjected to at the VA.

You can help build a powerful voice for the good of Veterans and the VA as well. We have set up Message Boards at WWW.PTSDHotline.Com for all of us to interact on.

You can now be part of a worldwide message board community of veterans pulling together to make positive changes in the VA System. The important keyword here is **Positive!**

With over 15 years of experience running message boards we will make sure that these boards are positive exchanges that will also benefit the VA.

Here is a link to the message boards: http://www.ptsdhotline.com/forum/forum.php

Go there. Set up an account and say Hi. Ask your questions and get answers. Help your

Veteran brothers and sisters build an interactive community where we can pool our energies to make positive changes in how we wish to be treated by our Government Agencies!

This is a perfect place to stay connected to other vets:

Vets Helping Vets

Did this guide help you in any way?

One more thing I would like to ask of you. If you liked or disliked the information in this guide please email me your thoughts. I will be making changes to this guide periodically and will use your input to try to help as many Vets as possible including myself.

DonP@PTSDHotline.Com

Welcome home to all my brothers and sisters from all wars!

Don Parent

Charlie Company

1st/35th Infantry Regiment

Cacti

Vietnam 1967 – 1968

About the Author

Don Parent
Vietnam 1967 - 1968
Charlie Company
1st / 35th Infantry Regiment
Cacti

Don on the beach at South China Sea 1967
His infantry unit was working with a Tank
Company for a few days.
That always made for a good night's sleep!
His first Purple Heart happened the next day.
The tanks didn't help enough!

Don Parent is a Writer, Website publisher, Internet Pioneer and Warzone PTSD Survivor. He is also a 100% Service Connected Disabled Vietnam veteran.

He was wounded five times leading up to and including the Tet Offensive of 1968. This resulted in multiple Purple Hearts. Four of the wounds happened in just one day. That was his last day in the field. But it was not his last day in the trenches (Flashbacks). He had years of war related trauma still ahead!

Over the next 45 years Don struggled with PTSD & Substance Abuse. Through research and study he was able to turn his life around and become a **War Zone PTSD Survivor**!

He now lives a happy and productive life with Ginger, his wife of 45 years. They were married on his R & R during his deployment.

Ginger suffered her own brand of PTSD by contact. She was Don's **"Care Giver"** for all those years. This is an extremely common condition for a Veteran's spouse or significant other. Their scars are often buried deeper and harder to see.

This Warzone PTSD Survivors Guide is Don's way of helping other Veterans & their families cut down the 45 year learning curve he was forced to travel.

When he came home from war there wasn't this type of information available to veterans. The VA and the Veterans had to learn the hard way. They learned from each other. They had to come up with terms like PTSD because nobody knew what was causing the uniquely similar problems so many vets were experiencing.

He believes your journey through recovery can be reduced from over 40 years to just months. It may take a few years to allow the steps & tools like Grounding Techniques to become automatic but the info in this guide can start making improvements in your life from day one!

Don & Ginger live in the High Desert of California. They have two married daughters and two granddaughters.